The Hemlock Dialogues

Imagining Socrates's Final Thoughts

I0522168

Stan Baronett

ALINEA

Alinea Learning

ALINEA

Alinea Learning

Boston, Massachusetts

Published in the United States by Alinea Learning, an imprint and division of Alinea Knowledge, LLC, Boston.

Visit our website at www.alinealearning.com.

Library of Congress Cataloging-in-Publication Data is available on file.

Print book ISBN: 979-8-9878531-5-3

eBook ISBN: 979-8-9878531-6-0

Cover photo: From Frontispiece, Harvard Classics, Volume II, published in 1910.

PREFACE

The Hemlock Dialogues imagines Socrates's final thoughts as he lay dying in his cell after drinking the cup of hemlock. *It is, therefore, a work of fiction.*

The book imagines Socrates's final reveries as they blaze through his mind, flitting from one setting to another as he nears death. An important goal was to show Socrates as a simple and honest man. It does this by recreating conversations in which Socrates subjects other people's ideas to examination. But it also reveals Socrates's acknowledgment that his own ideas need to be subjected to self-examination, which is the hallmark of Socrates's life.

This recreation lets readers see Socrates as an open and generous thinker, not as one who has all the final answers. Imagining Socrates's final internal thoughts charts a new landscape in which to explore some of his most important conversations.

When the jailer entered the cell carrying the cup of hemlock, Socrates said, "My good friend, since you are experienced in these matters, please give me directions how I am to proceed." The jailer answered, "After you drink the potion you simply have to walk around until your legs start to feel heavy, then lie down and the poison will act." Socrates took the cup, raised it to his lips, and drank the poison. Seeing his friends becoming quite emotional, Socrates said, "In order for me to die in peace, please be still and have patience."

Following the advice of the jailer, Socrates walked slowly around the cell until his legs began to fail, then he lay down on his back. After a short while, the jailer pressed Socrates's foot and asked if he could feel anything. "No," said Socrates. Little by little the numbness spread upward through Socrates's legs. "When the poison reaches the heart, that will be the end." Socrates's last spoken words were, "Crito, I owe a small debt to Asclepius; will you see that it is paid?" Crito assured him that he would, and asked Socrates if there was anything else. There was no answer.

≈ ≈ ≈ I listened carefully as my accusers made amazing claims against me; but nothing of what they said is true. I was particularly intrigued by their warning the jurors not to be seduced by the force of my eloquence. I'm surprised they can say that and not blush, because as soon as I begin presenting my defense you will see that I lack the ability to deceive. My simply telling the truth to you will be the only eloquence I have. You will hear the whole truth, spoken in simple terms, without the adornment of flowery phrases that distract the mind from sound judgement. Since I will present arguments that go directly to the heart of the matter under consideration, all I ask is that you grant me one favor. If you hear me using the same words in my defense that I have been in the habit of using everyday, then don't be surprised. I am over seventy years of age and, since this is the first time I have appeared in a court of law, I am a stranger to the ways of the court. I ask you to think only of the justice of my cause, and since I swear to speak truthfully, you must swear to decide justly.

There have been many accusers in my life, and their false accusations started long ago. They claimed that I was a skeptic who used fallacious reasoning, and that I taught others how to win an argument at any cost, and that I did not care about right and wrong and justice and injustice. These long-time accusers are the ones I dread most because I cannot question them here. I'm sure that some of them are among those who serve as jurors in this trial. So be it. I can fight only with their shadows, and pose questions when there is no one to answer.

To begin, let me say that if someone has the ability to teach, then I honor that person for being paid. But there is no truth to the claim that I am a teacher who takes money for instruction. In fact, I have nothing to teach anyone. Now probably some of you will say, *"But then, Socrates, where did these accusations against you originate? All this talk about you would never have arisen if you had been like other men."* I regard this as a fair challenge, and I will try to explain to you the origin of my evil fame.

If you ask me what wisdom I have, I reply, a wisdom that is attainable by any human. I refer you to a witness who is worthy of credit, and who will tell you about my wisdom—whether I have any, and of what sort—and that witness is the god Apollo. Some of you are already familiar with the story. But for those who are unaware of it, the story will provide not only an explanation for my public behavior, it will also reveal my reverence toward Apollo.

What happened was that my friend, Chaerephon, went to The Temple of Apollo at Delphi and asked the Oracle about me. According to the Oracle, Apollo decreed that no human was more honest, more temperate, or wiser than me. Since I hear many murmurs of dissent among the jurors, perhaps my story shocks some of you; some probably disbelieve it, while others react out of envy that I, among all men, should receive such praise from Apollo. If what she said was true, then it shouldn't be doubted. But as we all know, sometimes the Oracle speaks in riddles. If so, then perhaps I needed to find a way to

7

solve the riddle to reveal the full meaning of it. But how should I proceed? I decided to use the pronouncement as a guide to my actions in my daily conversations. I would investigate, point by point, what Apollo meant.

When many of my friends heard about the Oracle's pronouncement, they claimed that the characteristics mentioned were not couched in a riddle at all. *"As far as the first point, Socrates,"* they said, *"no one is more honest than you in your dealing with others. Further, no one is less enslaved than you to the appetites of the body. And no one is wiser because you are always willing to listen to anyone's opinion, and are eager to learn from anyone who claims to have knowledge. Those who make virtue, wisdom, and justice their pursuit choose to associate with you. Many people purchase delicacies of the market at great cost, but you, Socrates, are content with the delicacies of virtue, knowledge, and wisdom."*

Of course, it is always gratifying to hear praise from those who know you intimately. But whether their opinions are true is another matter; one that I needed to test for myself. You might ask why, if I accepted Apollo's decree as true, did I need to pursue it further? Again, I could not get it out of my mind that the Oracle might have posed Apollo's decree as a riddle. The ironic part is that my effort to solve the riddle is why I have such an evil reputation.

After long deliberation, I was able to think of a method to understand the riddle. I considered two points. First, the Oracle said that I was the wisest human of all. Second, I firmly believed that I was not wise. Imagine that you were in my position; wouldn't you be puzzled by this result? And wouldn't you think that perhaps the Oracle's answer shouldn't be taken literally? I see some heads nodding in agreement. Therefore, my course of action was clear. If I could find even one person wiser than me, then the true meaning of the Oracle's pronouncement might finally be revealed. If I found someone wiser than myself, then I would go to Apollo with a refutation in my hand. I would say to him, *"Here is someone who is wiser than I am; but you said that I was the wisest."* Perhaps my honest and determined pursuit would get Apollo to reveal the answer to the riddle.

My first step in the investigation was to go to a politician who had a reputation for being wise—his name I need not mention. The result was that when I began to talk with him, I could not help thinking that he was not really wise, although he was thought wise by many, and wiser still by himself. So, I explained to him that although he thought himself wise, he was not really wise. As you can imagine, the consequence was that he hated me, and his hatred was shared by several others who were present and heard me. I left him, saying to myself as I went away, *"Although I do not suppose that either of us knows anything, I am better off than he is because he knows nothing, but thinks that he knows, while I neither know nor think that I know."* It struck me that perhaps this was the answer to the riddle. Maybe what Apollo meant was that I am wise simply because I neither know nor think that I know, while others delude themselves into thinking that they know when they clearly do not know. It is in this, then, that I seem to have the advantage of others. Perhaps this is the particular wisdom that Apollo meant.

Although this was a good start to my pursuit, I couldn't stop because there were so many others to seek out for their purported knowledge. I went to someone who had a high philosophical reputation, but my conclusion was exactly the same as with the politician. Sadly, but perhaps not unexpectedly, I made another life-long enemy. Not wanting to give up in my search, I went to one person after another, not realizing the full extent and depth of the animosity I had provoked. But what else could I do? After all, the word of a god should be our first consideration. Who among you would denigrate a pronouncement by Apollo? Your shaking heads tell the answer. All who proclaim reverence to the gods would do exactly as I did. If not, you would be rejecting the possibility of a just and honorable life.

I resolved to seek out all those who had a reputation for knowledge, to find out the true meaning of the Oracle. And I swear to you—for I must tell you the truth—the result of my mission was that I found those with the greatest reputations were the most foolish. As you can imagine, my investigations over the years led to my having many enemies of the worst and most dangerous kind.

I am aware that a few people believe I am wise. They imagine, incorrectly, that I have a wisdom that I find lacking in others. I came to realize that what the Oracle meant was that the wisdom of humans is little or nothing. Therefore, when the Oracle mentioned me, she was using my name as an illustration, as if she said, *"He is the wisest, who, like Socrates, knows that his wisdom is in truth worth nothing."* And so I have gone my way, obedient to Apollo, and I continue to question the wisdom of anyone who appears to be wise. If it turns out that he is not wise, then in vindication of the Oracle, I show him that he is not wise. As you can imagine, this occupation takes up all my time; so much so, that I have no time to give to public matters or even to my own well-being. Consequently, I am in utter poverty by reason of my devotion to the task assigned to me.

There is another thing. Young men of the richer classes, who have not much to do, follow me around of their own free will. They enjoy hearing the pretenders of wisdom examined, and they often imitate me and examine others themselves. They quickly see that there are plenty of people who think they know something, but really know little or nothing. Of course, those who are examined and exposed by the young often end up being angry with me. They yell, *"This evil Socrates is a villainous corrupter of youth!"*

It is unfortunate that our society has been experiencing political upheavals, severe infighting, and political instability for a number of years. Perhaps some of you firmly believe that I have contributed to these states of affairs, so you want to use this trial as a pretense to eliminate my so-called influence. But that belief is unwarranted, misguided,

11

and false. If anyone here believes I have a malicious influence on society, then I ask you to come forward and tell us what evil I practice or teach. No one? I'm not surprised. They are incapable of giving even one example of my so-called malicious influence, or explain how it led to our society's difficult times. But this cowardly behavior is not new. The malicious influence of which I am falsely accused of displaying in my public conversations is really created by my accusers hiding in the shadows, far away from public scrutiny. But in order not to appear stupid, they repeat the same false charges which are used against all philosophers. When someone's ignorance is exposed, he attacks the philosopher. This is the truth and the whole truth. I have concealed nothing and I have not misled you. And yet I know that my plain speaking makes some people despise me. But their hatred is proof that I am speaking the truth.

I have said enough in my defense against the first group of my accusers. I turn now to the second group represented by Meletus, that good and patriotic man—as he calls himself. This is what he says: *"Socrates does evil by corrupting our youth; he does not believe in the gods of the state, and in fact has invented new gods of his own."* That is the nature of the accusations.

Let me say a few words about the accusations. Meletus claims that I do not believe in the gods of the state. This claim is instantly refuted by my reverence to Apollo, which I have told you about, and which I displayed in my daily search for someone wiser than me. Meletus also claims that I invented new gods. This accusation probably stems from my telling people that a voice warns me when I am about to do something wrong. Is this grounds for indictment? Many of those present have claimed that a sudden bird cry or a clap of thunder was a sign from the gods telling them what to do. The irony is that these are the same people who now want to condemn me for merely taking the advice of an inner voice whose only goal is to keep me from acting unjustly. Some of you may simply disbelieve what I say about the voice; others may be angry and jealous that I should receive more advice from the gods than they do. I have simply told the truth, and no matter where it leads, I have honored my duty to the court.

Meletus did not think of these charges by himself. He was influenced by others. In fact, many of you jurors are quite familiar with these charges after having seen them in the play *Clouds*, where the author, Aristophanes, introduces a buffoon, called "Socrates," going about and saying that he can walk in the air, and a great deal of other nonsense. We can laugh at the character in the play, but the charges of Meletus are no laughing matter. In fact, Meletus is the one who does evil because he makes a joke of a serious matter. He brought me to trial under false pretenses—from a fake interest about matters in which he is not really concerned. This I will prove to you. Meletus, come forward and let me ask you a question. Do you think a great deal about the improvement of the youth?

"Yes, I do."

Tell the jury, then, who improves the youth. After all, you must know, because you have taken great pains to discover and accuse their corrupter—me. Speak, then, and tell the judges and jury exactly who improves the youth. We are waiting patiently for your answer, Meletus. Alas, you are silent and have nothing to say. This is disgraceful, and it proves what I was saying—that you really have no interest in the matter. Speak up, friend, and tell us who improves the youth.

"The laws."

Thank you for respecting the court and finally offering a response. Unfortunately, your answer misses the point and avoids my meaning. Tell me specifically which persons know the laws.

"The judges who are present in court."

Do you mean they are able to instruct and improve the youth?

"Yes."

All of them, or some and not others?

"All of them."

Here is good news, indeed! There are plenty of improvers, then. And what do you say of the jurors—

do they improve the youth?

"Yes, they do."

And the senators?

"Yes."

But perhaps the members of the citizen assembly corrupt them? Or do they, too, improve the youth?

"They improve the youth."

Then every Athenian improves and elevates the youth. Everyone with the exception of myself. I am the lone corrupter. Is that what you affirm?

"That is what I strongly affirm."

Well then, that is unfortunate for me—if what you say is true. But suppose I ask you a question. Would you say that this also holds true in the case of horses? Does one person do them harm and all the rest of the world good? Isn't the exact opposite true? One person is able to do them good—the trainer of horses—while many others may injure them. Isn't that the truth? I see that you hesitate once again. Whether you say "*Yes*" or "*No*" doesn't matter. Now wouldn't it be great for the youth if they had only one corrupter, and all the rest of the world were their improvers. Unfortunately, by your ridiculous answers and ignorance, you have sufficiently shown

15

that you never really thought about the young. Your carelessness is seen in your lack of understanding, and your foolish attitude about the serious matters spoken of in this case. That much has been proven. But now I must ask you another question: Which is better—to live among bad citizens or among good ones? That is a question that even you can easily answer. Do the good citizens do their neighbors good, and the bad citizens do them evil?

"Yes."

And is there anyone who would rather be injured than benefited by those who live with him? Does anyone like to be injured?

"No."

And when you accuse me of corrupting the youth, do you allege that I corrupt them intentionally or unintentionally?

"Intentionally."

But you have just admitted that good people do their neighbors good, and evil people do them evil. Is that a truth which your superior wisdom has recognized early in life, and am I, at my age, so ignorant that I do not know that if I corrupt someone, then I am likely to be harmed by him in return—and yet I still intentionally corrupt him? If that is what you are saying, then I am afraid that you will not be able to persuade anyone. No, it is clear that I do not corrupt them intentionally, as you originally claimed. But perhaps you will amend your charge and now claim that I corrupt them unintentionally. But if that is the case, if my offence is unintentional, then you should have talked to me privately and warned me that my unintentional actions might prove harmful to the youth. If you had advised me, then I would have left off doing what I did purely unintentionally. But you did not warn me or teach me. Instead, you indicted me in this court, which is not a place of instruction, but of punishment. So, Meletus, your own statements under cross-examination show that you did not really care about the youth enough to talk to me about it. Nevertheless, I should still like to know in what regard you affirm that I corrupt the young. If we infer from your indictment, it is that I teach them not to acknowledge the gods recognized by the state, but instead, some other new divinities or spiritual agencies. These are the lessons which corrupt the youth, as you say.

"Yes, I say that emphatically."

Then, by all the gods of whom we are speaking, tell me and the court, in clear and direct terms, what you mean. Do you assert that I teach people to acknowledge some gods and, therefore, I do believe in gods, or you mean to say that I am an atheist and a teacher of atheism?

"I mean the latter—that you are a complete

17

atheist."

That is an extraordinary statement. Do you really think that I do not believe in any god?

> *"I swear by Zeus that you believe absolutely in none at all."*

I'm sorry to say, but once again you are a liar, Meletus, and even you don't believe what you are saying. I cannot help thinking that you are simply reckless and impudent, and that you have written this indictment in a spirit of mere wantonness and youthful bravado. Did you say to yourself, *"I shall see whether this wise Socrates will discover my ingenious contradiction, or whether I shall be able to deceive him and the court."* For it appears that you contradict yourself in the indictment, since you said that Socrates is guilty of not believing in the gods, and yet he believes in them. It is easy to reveal your inconsistency. I simply have to ask you the following. Do you think that anyone believes both in the existence of humans and not in the existence of humans? Or does anyone believe in horsemanship, but not in horses? Or in flute-playing, but not in flute-players? Please speak up. Oh, so once again, you have no answer. Don't worry, I'll answer for you, since you obviously refuse to answer for yourself. No, Meletus, no one ever believed those things. So now, let's see if you are willing to answer the next question. Can someone believe in spiritual and divine agencies, but not in spirits or demigods?

"He cannot."

I am glad that I have extracted that answer, even though it required the assistance of the court to drag it out of you. Now, Meletus, you have sworn in the indictment that I teach and believe in spiritual agencies. But if I believe in divine beings, then I must believe in spirits or demigods, isn't that true? Yes, that is true, for I may assume that your silence means that you agree. Now what are spirits or demigods? Aren't they either gods or the children of gods?

"Yes, they are."

Good, then this is just the contradiction of which I was speaking. It is obvious that spirits and demigods are gods. But you assert, first, that I don't believe in gods and I am an atheist, and, second, that I do believe in gods. In other words, if I believe in demigods, and if demigods are the illegitimate children of gods, then this necessarily implies the existence of their parents. You might as well affirm the existence of mules, and deny that of horses and donkeys. Such nonsense, Meletus, could have been intended by you only as a trial of my intelligence and that of the court. You have put this into the indictment because you had nothing real of which to accuse me. But no one who has a particle of understanding will ever be convinced by you that the same person can believe in divine and spiritual beings and yet not believe that there are gods and demigods. As we have seen, simple reasoning is enough to refute your charges as being illogical.

I have said enough in answer to the charges of Meletus. His own foolish answers to my questions reveal the emptiness of his accusations against me. In light of what has just happened, I ask the jurors to consider whether my cross-examination of Meletus corrupted him in any way. My questions revealed the truth and exposed the accusations as false. When truth is revealed, is anyone corrupted? In fact, everyone believes that truth is liberating, and it is something that our powers of reasoning can help us discover, but only if we apply it consistently and conscientiously. This is the path that I took in my public discussions.

As I said earlier, I have many enemies whose hatred has led to the death of many good men, and will probably be the death of many more. There is no danger of my possibly being the last of them. Perhaps some of you are saying to yourself, *"Aren't you ashamed, Socrates, for leading a life that is likely to bring you to an untimely end?"* My response is that this view is mistaken. We should not spend our lives trying to calculate our chances of living or dying—we should consider only whether our actions are right or wrong. Whatever we do, whatever our place in society, whether that place is chosen or thrust upon us, there we should remain in the hour of danger. We should not think of death, but only of disgrace.

Of course, my conduct could be criticized if I first agreed to follow the Oracle's pronouncement, but later abandoned my mission through fear of being punished. If I disobeyed Apollo because I was afraid of death, then I could rightfully be accused of irreverence. In that case, you would be justified in bringing me to court for denying the existence of the gods. The fear of death is the pretense of wisdom, not real wisdom, because it assumes a knowledge of the unknown. No one knows whether death, which most fear to be the greatest evil, may in fact be the greatest good. And this is the point in which I might perhaps think myself wiser than others: Whereas I know nothing of the afterworld, I do not pretend that I know.

I do know, however, that injustice is evil and dishonorable. Suppose you reject the suggestion of my accusers who said that if I were not put to death, then your children will all be utterly ruined by listening to my words. Suppose, instead, that you let me go, and say to me, *"Socrates, this time we will not listen to your accusers. We will let you off, but on one condition—that you are not to inquire and converse with others in this way any longer, and that if you are caught doing this again you shall die."* If this were the condition on which you let me go, I would reply as follows: Although I honor and love you, I shall obey god rather than you, and while I have life and strength I shall never cease from the practice of philosophy. I will continue to ask citizens why they are so concerned with attaining the greatest amount of money, glory, and power, but are so little concerned with wisdom, truth, and improving their souls and characters. And if the person with whom I am talking says, *"But I do care about those things,*

Socrates," then I will continue to question him. And this I will do to everyone I meet—young or old, citizen or not—because this is what I have been commanded to do. I do nothing but go about persuading the old and young alike, not to think first about their possessions, but instead of improving their characters. I assert that virtue is not acquired through money, but that from virtue comes everything good, public as well as private. This is my mission, and if this is the doctrine which corrupts the youth, then my influence is ruinous indeed. But if anyone says that this is not my mission, then he is speaking an untruth. Thus, I say to you, either acquit me or not; but whatever you do, know that I shall never alter my ways, not even if I have to die many times.

I hear some murmurs of disapproval among you, and see some bodies shifting uncomfortably in their seats. Please hear me out. I want you to know that, if you kill me, then you will injure yourselves more than me. The greatest evil is to take away another person's life unjustly. So, I am not going to argue for my own sake, but for yours, that you may not sin against god and truth. If you kill me, you will not easily find another like me, who, if I may use such a ludicrous figure of speech, am a gadfly that has been given to the state. In this regard, the state is like a great and noble horse who is slow in his motions, owing to his great size, and he requires to be stirred into life. I am the gadfly who spends all his time landing on you, biting, annoying, and provoking you into action.

You may say to me, *"But Socrates, by your own analogy we know that flies can definitely be annoying, and they do arouse us, at least enough to shoo them away. But, if we are really annoyed, we kill them."* My response is that since you will not easily find another like me, I would advise you to spare me. Yes, you may feel irritated at being suddenly awakened when you are caught napping, and you may think that if you were to strike me dead, which you might easily do, then you would sleep on for the remainder of your lives—unless god in his infinite wisdom gives you another gadfly. And that I am given to you by god is shown by this: If I had been like other men, then I would not have neglected my own wellbeing. Instead, I have been coming to you individually, like a father or elder brother, pleading with you to regard virtue. My behavior is not typical. Now if I had gained anything, or if I had been paid, then there would have been some sense in the accusations against me. But not even the impudence of my accusers dares to say that I have ever exacted or sought payment from anyone. They have no witness of that. But I have the best witness of the truth of what I say—my poverty is my witness. Even here where my life is at stake, I will not abandon my mission to help whoever I meet. My defense in this trial has been a consistent illustration of my mission: To stir people to think about important things fairly, honestly, and justly, even if they might not want to.

If anyone says that he has ever heard anything from me in private which all the world has not heard,

I should like you to know that he is speaking an untruth. You might ask, *"But why do people delight in continually conversing with you, Socrates?"* I have already told you the truth about this, but let me repeat: Some people like to hear the cross-examination of the pretenders to wisdom—there can be amusement in this. But that is not why I do it. Do not forget that I am merely following a duty which Apollo has imposed upon me, and which I take seriously. As I said earlier, if I am really corrupting the youth, and have corrupted some of them already, then those who have grown up and have realized that I gave them bad advice in the days of their youth can come forward as accusers and take their revenge. I ask them again to come forth and swear to the court. Once again, observe that no one steps forward. Then perhaps some of the relatives of those I supposedly corrupted will be willing to relate the evil their families suffered at my hands. Now is their time. Let them present themselves as witnesses against me. As you have seen repeatedly, no one comes forward to testify against me because they know that I am speaking the truth, and that my accusers are lying.

You have heard me speak in my defense. Now some of you might be surprised that I have not produced my family in court to move you with tears. I will not bring any of them here in order to petition you for an acquittal. Why not? Not from any self-will or disregard of you. Whether I am or am not afraid of death is another question, of which I will not now speak. But my reason is simply that I feel such conduct to be discreditable to myself, and to you, and the whole state. Someone who has reached my years should not debase himself. At any rate, the world seems to have decided that Socrates is in some way wiser than other men. And if those among you who are said to be wise, courageous, and virtuous, have demeaned themselves by parading tearful relatives on your behalf, then your conduct was shameful. I have seen men of great reputation, when they have been condemned, behaving in the strangest manner. They seemed to fancy that they were going to suffer something dreadful if they died, and that they would be immortal if you allowed them to live. This behavior dishonors the state. But, setting aside the question of dishonor, there seems to be something wrong in winning acquittal by means other than convincing arguments and evidence. Thus, you should not expect me to do what I consider dishonorable and irreverent, especially now, when I am being tried for irreverence. If by sheer force of emotional persuasion I could overpower your oath for determining the truth, then the accusers would be correct. But that is not the case. I believe that we are capable of using reason to arrive at the truth by the weight of convincing arguments and evidence, as I have shown throughout my defense. Now it is in your hands. ≈ ≈ ≈

≈ ≈ ≈ I am not surprised by the vote to find me guilty. Based on the long-standing animosity of many in attendance, I expected it. I am surprised only that the votes are so nearly equal. I had thought that the majority against me would be far larger. If, however, thirty votes out of the five hundred cast had gone over to the other side, I would have been acquitted.

My accusers propose death as the penalty. What shall I propose? Clearly that which is my due. And what is it that I should pay or receive? What shall be done to someone who has been careless of what so many care about—wealth, family interests, and political power? Reflecting that I was too honest to live that way, I went where I could do the greatest good privately to everyone of you. I tried to persuade you to look into yourself—to seek virtue and wisdom before you look to your private interests.

Now you need to determine what should be done to me. Given how I devoted my life trying to make people more virtuous, I should receive my just reward. What would be a reward suitable to a poor man who is your benefactor, who desires only leisure that he may converse with you? There can be no more fitting reward than to be provided with free meals in the state dining room, the place reserved for the most distinguished citizens. Based on the clamor among you, it seems that many think my proposal impudent or insulting to the court. But I assure you that since I never intentionally wronged anyone, I will not wrong myself. Therefore, I will not say of myself that I deserve any punishment, or propose any penalty. Do you think I am afraid of the death penalty which has been proposed? Why should I be, when I do not know whether death is a good or a bad thing.

Should I propose imprisonment for myself? But why should I live in prison and be the slave of temporary rulers? What if I say exile, which is possibly the penalty that I will receive from you? Well, then I must indeed be blinded by the love of life if I were to consider that since you, who are my own citizens, cannot put up with me, others are more likely to embrace me. And what a strange life I would lead, at my age, wandering from city to city, living in constant exile.

Now, in exasperation, someone among you will surely say, *"Socrates, no one will interfere with you if you simply learn to hold your tongue!"* I know it may be difficult to make you understand my answer. If I tell you that doing so would be a disobedience to a divine command—something that I will not do—then you will not believe I am serious. If I insist that the greatest good is to converse about virtue, and that the unexamined life is not worth living, then you will still not believe me. And yet what I say is true, and the truth leads to the conclusion that I do not deserve any punishment. But I suspect by your demeanor that the truth is not enough to persuade many of you. So be it. The fault lies in your character, not mine. I leave it in your hands once again. ≈ ≈ ≈

≈ ≈ ≈ Since you have voted to condemn me to death, allow me to make a final statement. There are those who will criticize your judgment, who will say that you killed Socrates, a wise man. They will call me wise even though I am not wise, simply because they will want to condemn your decision against me. So let me speak now to those of you who have condemned me to death. If only you had waited a little while, your desire would have been fulfilled in the course of nature. For I am old and not far from death. You think that I was convicted through a deficiency of words, that I did not do enough to gain an acquittal. That is not so. The deficiency which led to my conviction was not of words or clear arguments. Rather it was because I did not address you as you would have liked me to address you— weeping and wailing and saying and doing many things which you have been accustomed to hear from others—and which, as I say, are unworthy of an honest person. Of course, there are many ways of escaping death, if someone is willing to say and do anything. The difficulty is not in avoiding death, but in avoiding unrighteousness, for that runs faster than death, and I am old and move slowly. And to those who have condemned me, I will make a prediction. I am about to die, and that is the hour in which people are sometimes gifted with prophetic power. I prophesy to you who are my murderers, that after my death, punishment far heavier than you have inflicted on me will surely await you. Me you have killed because you wanted to escape your examiner, so not to have to account for your lives. But you will face many more examiners. If you think that by killing me you can avoid criticism of your lives, then you are sadly mistaken. That is not a way of escape which is either possible or honorable. The noblest way is not to crush others, but to improve yourselves.

Now, to those friends who voted to acquit me, I would like to talk with you about what has happened. I should like to show you the meaning of this event, and tell you of a wonderful circumstance. There has come upon me that which is generally believed to be the last and worst evil. But today, the inner voice that gives me advice made no attempt to stop me, either as I was leaving my house, or when I was going to court, or while I was speaking, or at anything that I was going to say. And yet, I have often been stopped in the middle of a conversation—but today, nothing I either said or did in court was blocked by the voice. I am not surprised that many people are apt to misunderstand what I mean by the voice that I hear, because I sometimes do not know quite how to understand it myself. I do not hear a voice whose sound is different from my own except that it is inside me and does not come through my ears as it would if I were speaking out loud. And it never tells me directly that what I am doing is right; instead, I hear it only when I am about to do something wrong. It acts like a warning device to keep me from doing some injustice to myself or others. It whispers to me to think carefully about what I am about to do. It nudges me to ponder the consequences of my actions and words. It may be simply one part of my thinking and reasoning process that asks me to look further into what follows from what I am about to do. We all think to ourselves, and sometimes we talk to ourselves out loud. My voice might simply be me talking to myself. But if so, it is the best part of me that offers good counsel. What do I take to be the explanation of this? I will tell you. I regard this as evidence that what has happened to me is simply an unfortunate consequence of my consistently telling the truth. I am the victim of unjust and dishonorable men, not a victim of the truth.

If we look at it objectively, we will see that there is reason to believe that death is not to be feared. Either death is a state of nothingness and utter unconsciousness, or else there is a migration of the spirit from this world to another. Now, if you believe there is no consciousness after death, that it is a sleep undisturbed even by dreams, then death will be an unspeakable gain. If a person were to select the night in which his sleep was undisturbed, and then were to tell us how many days and nights he had passed in the course of his life more pleasantly than that one, I think he will not find many such days or nights. If death is like this, then I say that to die is a gift, for eternity is then merely a single night.

On the other hand, if death is the journey to another place, and there we will meet all those who have once lived, then what could be greater than that? If we meet people who were righteous during their life, then the journey will be worth making. And who would not want to converse with the greatest philosophers and poets? If this is true, then let me die again and again. Above all, I shall be able to continue my search for wisdom. I shall find out who is wise, and who pretends to be wise and is not. For in that world they do not put a man to death for this.

I have one last favor to ask of you my friends—to carry on my work. Question those who seem to care about riches more than about virtue; criticize them for not caring about that for which they ought to care. It is much easier to pursue immediate gratification, to seek fame and transitory rewards, than it is to follow reason wherever it takes us, and to question our motives and beliefs. I know how difficult it is to strive for knowledge, virtue, and wisdom, but If you spend your life asking the right questions, then you honor me. And if you do this, I and my family will have received justice.

The hour of departure has arrived and we go our separate ways—I to die, and you to live. Who can say with certainty which is better? ≈ ≈ ≈

≈ ≈ ≈ Welcome to my humble cell. I will be here for the remainder of my life, which may last a few weeks or perhaps a month. The jailer takes care of me, and he allows visitors at any time. My family and you, my friends, bring me an abundance of food, although I don't require much.

I know that many of you are dismayed and disappointed at how I conducted my defense at the trial. Please, give voice to your concerns, so I can help you get past your doubts and anguish at the result.

"If you don't mind, Socrates, I have a question. Even after Meletus had drawn up

the indictment, you continued to discuss everything in your daily conversations except your impending trial. Shouldn't you have spent your time practicing your defense for the trial, and asking your friends for advice?"

I have been practicing my whole life, Hermogenes.

"What do you mean by that curious statement, Socrates?"

Quite simply that I have spent my life applying reason to understand what is just and what is unjust, and in my daily actions doing what is right and abstaining from what is wrong. The trial was simply a continuation of how I conducted my life, and, I believe, was the best defense possible.

"But didn't you understand Socrates, how common it is, even under the influence of sound arguments, that our juries condemn innocent people to death, and acquit actual criminals through pity or flattery?"

I assure you that each time I focused my thoughts on my defense, the inner voice counseled me.

"How strange that sounds, Socrates."

Not at all. I believe the voice was telling me not to think of devising ways to sway the jurors, but simply to tell the truth. I am content to believe that up to the present moment there is no person who has spent a better or happier life than mine. I regard as the best possible life that can be attained as one that is achieved by trying to become as virtuous and knowledgeable as possible in the short time we are here on earth. This has come to me through my accidental and fortuitous conversations with others.

If I had been allowed to live longer, then perhaps I would have been forced to pay in full the penalties of old age—to see and hear less keenly, to fail in intellectual force, and to leave school, as it were, more of a dunce than when I came, less learned and more forgetful. And if I became unable to recognize the impending changes, then my life left would scarcely be worth living, since, as I have said many times, the unexamined life is not one that I care to live. On the other hand, if I were conscious of the changes, but unable to stop them, then I would consider the existence left to me to be joyless, a death in life, devoid of life's charm.

Yet, since it has been reserved for me to die unjustly, then on those who unjustly convicted me lies the shame. The disgrace of an unjust verdict falls on them, not me. There is a long line of predecessors on this road, and their reputations vary according to whether they did wrong or suffered wrong. As for myself, I know that I shall obtain from mankind a consideration far different from that which will be accorded to those who put me to death. I know that undying witness will attest that I never at any time did wrong to anyone, or made anyone worse, but forever tried to make those who were with me better persons.

Did I purposely try to lose my case at the trial? Did I try to antagonize the jurors, knowing they would sentence me to death? Perhaps part of me did think that I had lived long enough, that I didn't want to grow so old and infirm that I was a burden to myself and others, that I didn't want to lose the power of reason. After all, most people at some time in their life think about their death, and some even contemplate suicide, although I argued against it. But our minds contemplate many things, quite often without any conscious direction, whereby the strangest ideas occur to us, however fleetingly. No, my friends, I presented my case as another example of how I presented myself to everyone on a daily basis. By my actions did I in fact commit suicide? Anyone who truly knows me would have to agree: That I would not do.

One might as well ask, *"Did you go to war, Socrates, because you wanted to die?"* No, I went to war and fought the enemy hoping to survive the battles, but I did it honorably. By that I mean if I had gone to war unwillingly, then I might have tried to avoid battle at whatever cost. But if I went willingly, thinking it was my duty to protect my country, then I would fight to the best of my ability and use whatever tactics I could muster to survive.

Perhaps you might say to me, *"But Socrates, the circumstances of war are far different from a court of law."* Granted there are important differences. At my trial, I accepted the laws, did not disparage the proceedings, and defended myself honorably, as I pointed out repeatedly in court. I treated the jurors exactly as I did all those with whom I came into contact. My conversation with the jurors was meant to be a personal conversation, so it contained the same reasoning process as any of my one-on-one encounters. I spoke the truth. I exposed Meletus as a liar. I revealed to the jurors the same character that I displayed everyday. So, if I did not lie, flatter, or play the role of a sophist on a daily basis, then had I done any of those in court, I would have revealed myself as a hypocrite, as someone desperate to be acquitted under false pretenses. That I would not do.

Perhaps someone accustomed to making wagers on the outcomes of games of chance, and who was privy to how I would conduct my defense, could have predicted that I would lose, be found guilty, and sentenced to death. And suppose that person begged me to change my tactics. Should I have listened to that advice? If being honest and telling the truth sometimes leads to bad results, should we then resort to dishonesty and lying? I was not willing to save my life at the cost of renouncing my integrity and character. It would have reduced my life to rubble and reveal me to be a charlatan. That I would not do.

It appears that discussions about my trial and its outcome continue to reverberate among you, my closest friends. Xenophon, you seem anxious to say something. Please do not hesitate to say anything that is on your mind.

"Socrates, you have never wearied of discussing questions that touch on everyday life and human actions. What do the terms 'piety,' 'impiety,' 'just' and 'unjust' mean? What is the proper role of a politician? Must we obey the laws? Why should I be good?

"I think we can all agree that anyone who obtains correct answers to these and other questions can truly said to have attained the mark of wisdom. Did anyone strive harder than Socrates to find those answers? Did anyone implore his fellow citizens to seek knowledge, to attain virtue, more than Socrates? And he did this throughout his life, long before many of us were even born. Since direct knowledge of Socrates's ideas was unknown to many Athenians, and since many jurors relied on unsubstantiated gossip and the false testimony of those who brought him to trial, it is not surprising that many jurors came to the wrong conclusion. If they truly wanted to remain objective and render a just verdict, then the relevant facts concerning the conduct of Socrates's life were easily available. However, too many jurors completely ignored the truth, and by so doing, renounced their sworn duty to render a just verdict.

"No less surprising is the pernicious belief that Socrates corrupted the young. Socrates kept his appetites and passions *under strict control; he was perfectly capable of enduring winter's cold and summer's heat. He was so dedicated to minimizing his personal needs that even with the scantiest of means he never asked for more. I ask you: Is it credible that such a man could have made others irreverent or lawless? Was he not rather the savior of many through the passion for virtue that he roused in them, and the hope he infused that through careful management of themselves they might grow to be truly good. He was an exemplar of virtue whose personal behavior toward others offered the purest illustration of what he tried to convey through words. The desire to imitate his virtuous behavior had a strong effect on many, including the young. How, I ask, can this be a corruption?*

"Least of all did he tend to make his companions greedy and to seek riches and power. Since he had many followers, he could have charged a fee for his lively and enlightening conversations—many would have gladly paid—but that he did not do. His behavior showed to everyone that important discussions about life were not to be debased by money or by teaching others the art of winning an argument by any means. The reward of reasoning should be a mutually honest search between friends. Socrates was content to believe that those who spent time in his company, and were

willing to apply reason to the hard questions of life, would continue to play their part as good and true friends to himself and one another throughout their lives. I ask once more then: How could a man of this character corrupt the young, unless the careful cultivation of virtue is corruption?"

Thank you for saying such things, Xenophon. Do you have anything else to add?

"Yes. In a short while Socrates will not be with us, so I want to remind those present not to forget some of the things we discussed with him. Socrates warned us that the capacity for honest reasoning and action cannot grow without a secure foundation of self-control—the virtues of temperance and discipline. Those who ignore the virtues are likely to become people drawn to power and injustice."

Thank you, Xenophon. As we reflect on the infinite diversity and beauty of nature, we can see that humans have been endowed with sensibilities which correspond to this diversity. For instance, the faculty of reasoning enables us to draw inferences concerning the things which we perceive, and by aid of memory to understand how each set of things may be turned to our good, and to devise countless tools for enjoying the good and repelling evil. Consider the faculty of speech, by which we can instruct one another and participate in all the forms of society, to establish laws, and to enter upon a civilized existence. But do not think that these gifts automatically lead to wisdom, knowledge, and virtue; those we must earn. And do not forget that our souls are hidden from our gaze. Do you wish to add anything, Xenophon?

"I do. Socrates never made a secret of his beliefs regarding justice and honesty. In fact, as many of you know, he routinely gave practical demonstrations of it, both in his private conversations with us and by his law-abiding and helpful behavior to all, whether in the life of the city or in his military service, such that a pattern of loyalty to the rest of the world was revealed. I will mention three such demonstrations.

"First, when Socrates was asked to lead the assembly in an important matter at a time of turmoil, when emotions were running high among the members, he made sure that the assembled body did not take an unconstitutional vote, but instead to remain on the side of the laws. Second, when the Thirty tried to lay some injunction on Socrates, contrary to the laws, he refused to obey, as for instance when they forbade him conversing with the young, or when they ordered him and certain other citizens to arrest a man to be put to death, he refused

> *on the ground that the injunctions were contrary to the laws. Third, when Socrates appeared as defendant in the suit instituted by Meletus, it was customary for litigants to flatter and appease the judges hoping for acquittal. But Socrates refused to perform any unseemly act, preferring to abide by the laws and die rather than transgress them and live."*

I see that many of you agree with Xenophon, but I suspect that some of you still want to discuss my trial, so please speak up.

> *"What Xenophon said is true. Based on the votes the majority of the five hundred jurors obviously agreed with the accusations. It may be that many believed that Socrates convinced his followers to despise the established laws. Socrates, please tell us why you failed to tell the jurors more about this topic."*

I suspect you refer to my habit of arguing about the process of appointing state officers by ballot, and how it is bound to fail whenever the majority of the citizens are ignorant of the issues and the characters of those seeking power. Of course, you might trust the majority of your neighbors to recommend a musician to play at a wedding, where a mistake would be far less disastrous than in electing a corrupt politician. Pointing out the potential mistakes and dangerous consequences in letting a simple majority decide important matters is likely to be threatening to those already in power, and insulting to citizens who thought their votes should count even if they had no idea of what they were voting for or against. But that should not stop us from telling the truth. How else can a corrupt system be changed, if not through rational arguments?

My accusers and enemies have long twisted my ideas. That is not something new. The only new thing is that they finally brought me to court. Perhaps they thought that in the current political climate their false accusations that I incited the young to be violent might sway enough jurors to find me guilty. It turns out they were correct. But we who know the truth know that my intent was to use reason to cultivate wisdom in everyone I met. That was the truth I spoke about in court. My hope is that some of you will continue to instruct our fellow-citizens to pursue knowledge, virtue, and wisdom, which is the least likely to lead to partisans of violence. Would anyone like to respond? Xenophon?

> *"Thank you, Socrates. Isn't it true that some of your severest accusers often referred to two men who brought great tragedies to the state—Critias and Alcibiades—who were your followers when they were young?"*

That is true. They spent time with me when they were young.

"You would not find a more arrant thief, savage, and murderer than Critias. And the master of insolence and high-handedness was Alcibiades. Those two wretched men wrought tremendous evil to the state, so I have no desire to appear as the apologist of either one. I confine myself to explaining what this intimacy of theirs with Socrates really was.

"When Critias and Alcibiades spent their time with Socrates, they were able, by his support, to suppress their dishonorable characters. In fact, as soon as they felt themselves to be better and smarter than everyone else, they left Socrates and plunged into the whirl of politics. Their swift subsequent actions are a conclusive witness that their true characters existed long before they met Socrates, and for which he cannot be responsible.

"As soon as he separated himself from Socrates's guidance, Critias went to Thessaly where he joined those well-versed in lawlessness. And Alcibiades fared no better. His attraction to those in political power soon exposed him to the allure of corruption. He quickly learned the skills of flattery and its results on the gullible, and being so sure of himself, he renounced any need for self-control and self-examination. Buoyed by his own inner unquestioned beliefs, he forgot all that he had previously

learned. Once on the road to power he was blind to other alternatives and refused to doubt his own ideas. His fanaticism took control and was fueled by an inflated pride of famous ancestry, exalted by wealth, puffed up by power, sapped to the soul's core by a host of human temptations. And once separated from Socrates's temperate and modest nature, is it any wonder that he reached the full stature of arrogancy? Is Socrates to be held responsible for the offences of these two arrogant men? Socrates's accusers should be embarrassed to claim that he was responsible. Instead, they refuse to acknowledge that when Critias and Alcibiades followed Socrates they were modest and well-behaved. Yet not one word of praise is uttered by the accusers for this.

"Should a teacher who has turned out proficient pupils be held to account because one of them goes away to another teacher and turns out to be a failure? Or what father, if he has a child who in the society of a certain friend remains an honest lad, but then by falling into the company of some other becomes a good-for-nothing, will that father straightway accuse the earlier instructor? Will not he rather, in proportion as the child deteriorates in the company of the latter, bestow more heartfelt praise upon the former? This would have been a

fair test to apply to Socrates: Was he guilty of any base conduct himself? If so, then let him be accused; but if, on the contrary, he never faltered in virtuous character, how in the name of justice is he to be held to account for a baseness which was in others and not in him?

"It is also true that when Socrates tried to show Critias that he was being led astray, Critias turned on him, and from that point on hated Socrates. When Critias was one of the Thirty, he framed the law against teaching the art of reasoning merely from a desire to vilify Socrates. To punish Socrates, he made the usual baseless charge that philosophers are dangerous, by which he hoped to get the public to fear Socrates. If you don't mind, Socrates, perhaps some of those among us do not know the full story. Do you mind talking about it?"

Not at all. At the time when the Thirty were putting citizens to death wholesale, I observed that it would be extraordinarily reckless if a cattle owner continually starved and killed his cattle, but a ruler of a state who was continually starving and killing the citizens, and who will not admit to be a horrible ruler, or even be ashamed of his actions, is even more reckless and reprehensible. When those remarks were reported back to Critias, he summoned me. Critias proceeded to point out the law against teaching the art of reasoning, and he forbade me to converse with the young. As is my custom, I asked Critias a question: Critias, I want to make sure that I fully understand what you mean when you forbid me to converse with the young. May I ask for a clarification?

"You may," replied Critias.

Thank you. I am prepared to obey the laws, but to avoid transgression of the law through ignorance, I need instruction. You order me to abstain from conversing with the young. But do you mean that the art of conversing leads to correct statements, or to incorrect statements? If the former, then must I abstain from speaking correctly? And if the latter, then should I endeavor to amend my speech?

> *"Given your obvious ignorance, Socrates, I will frame the prohibition in language better suited to your intelligence. Therefore, I forbid you to hold any conversation whatsoever with the young."*

Once again, in order to avoid all ambiguity, or the possibility of my doing anything than what you are pleased to command, may I ask you to define up to what age a human being is to be considered young?

> *"For just so long a time as he is debarred from sitting as a member of the Council, as not having attained to the maturity of*

wisdom. Accordingly you will not converse with anyone under the age of thirty."

So, if I wish to buy something, then I am not allowed to ask the price, if the vendor is under the age of thirty?

"Of course in situations of that kind you can talk to a person under the age of thirty. But here is the problem in a nutshell, Socrates. You have a maddening way of asking questions when all the while you know how the matter stands. So let us have no questions of that sort."

Thank you. But now I need to know if I am allowed to answer a young person's question. For example, suppose a young person asks me where I live, or what I had for dinner?

"Oh yes, of course, things of that kind are allowed. But at the same time you had better stop having conversations with shoemakers, carpenters, farmers, and shipbuilders, even those over the age of thirty."

So, I am barred from discussing topics such as justice, knowledge, reverence and the like?

"Absolutely. And from cattle owners in particular, or else see that you do not lessen the number of the herd yourself."

My friends, you can see by this retelling of the meeting that my earlier remark about cattle owners and rulers had been relayed to Critias who could not forgive me for saying it. As soon as they obtained the power they craved, Critias and Alcibiades turned their backs on me. They now found my manner of living unattractive, not to speak of the annoyance of being cross-examined about their own obvious shortcomings.

If you wish to see my true companions you should look to Crito, Chaerephon, Hermogenes, Simmias, and others, who stay with me and who continue striving to attain virtuous characters and knowledge in order to manage the various duties of life, to house and family, to relatives and friends, to fellow-citizens, and to the state at large. Of these true followers not one in youth or old age was ever guilty, or thought guilty, of committing any evil deed.

Now if you don't mind, I would like to discuss a topic that is relevant to what has happened since my trial, but which has gone unspoken: The question of freedom. This is important because many of you believe that freedom has been taken away from me by the verdict. Tell me, do you believe freedom to be a noble and magnificent acquisition, whether for an individual or for a state?

> *"I cannot conceive of a nobler or more magnificent acquisition, Socrates."*

Then do you believe a person to be a free who is ruled by the pleasures of the body, and thereby cannot perform what is best?

"No."

To have something over you that will prevent you doing what is best is a loss of freedom?

"Yes."

It hinders us from doing things which will be useful and beneficial. It drags us toward things which are merely and temporarily pleasant, and away from the cultivation of the virtues that create stable and long-lasting behavior. Given this, is it reasonable to suppose that self-control is a necessary ingredient to attaining wisdom?

"Yes, that is a natural inference."

Then is self-control the path to the highest pleasures?

"I don't follow you, Socrates. Can you explain your meaning?"

The lack of self-control causes a person to be unable to resist hunger and thirst, or the allure of sexual desires, or the desire to sleep too long, or the easy paths to procrastination. In contrast, self-control enables us to avoid those traps. It gives us the power to control any pleasure worth remembering.

"Are you saying, Socrates, that anyone who is controlled by the pleasures of the body has no concern at all with virtue?"

A person who foregoes all chance of improvement, who seeks only to gratify his sense of pleasure, has also given up the possible discovery of the greatest treasures that are attained through knowledge and wisdom. We reach the zenith of our existence by maximizing our use of reason, the most precious gift we have. The term "discussion" means people coming together in honest deliberation to share ideas and challenge each other to clarify our thoughts. For example, if someone has knowledge of a particular matter, then he will be able to explain this knowledge to others. But someone who does not have that particular knowledge will stumble and fail to explain it.

We need to understand specific instances and practical cases where we feel confident that our ideas stand up under scrutiny. Determining how complex ideas can be understood partly through real-life situations may lead to a greater universal understanding of the important concepts. ≈ ≈ ≈

≈ ≈ ≈ *"Our visits to your cell are meant to cheer you up, Socrates, so don't feel obligated to engage us the way you would if we were meeting in the marketplace where we would discuss some topic that was on our minds."*

My present location does not dictate the way I conduct my life, no matter how short or long the time I have left, so please, Hippias, ask me whatever you wish.

"Thank you, Socrates. I know you have already talked about certain topics in the past, but speaking for myself, I don't always grasp the nuances of your arguments, or if I think I do, then when I try to reconstruct it later on I find myself struggling to retrace the steps. For example, can you clarify what you mean by 'a just person,' and what 'justice' means?"

I never tire of discussing these topics. The ability to clarify what we mean is crucial for others to understand what we believe, and how those beliefs underpin and justify our actions. This is especially true for actions that can result in serious consequences. Let me illustrate this by telling you of a chance meeting I had with Euthyphro before my trial:

"Socrates, what are you doing here at the court? I know that you would never bring a lawsuit against anyone, so either you or a relative must be the subject of a legal

proceeding."

You are correct, Euthyphro. In fact, I have recently been indicted.

"What? Who brought charges against you, Socrates?"

A young man named Meletus.

"What are the charges?"

Something quite serious. Meletus claims that the youth of Athens are being corrupted, and that I am corrupting them. He also accuses me of inventing new gods and denying the existence of old ones—these are the grounds of his indictment.

"Those are old complaints by those who felt embarrassed and offended by your cross-examination techniques. Others are jealous that you have a reputation for being wise. But Meletus is clever, since he knows that many people will readily respond to such charges."

Our fellow Athenians do not trouble themselves about someone who is thought to be wise, until that person begins to impart his wisdom to others, and then for some reason or other they become angry.

"I am never likely to tempt their anger,"

remarked Euthyphro.

Of course not. You are reserved in your behavior, and seldom impart your wisdom. But, as you know, I have a habit of opening myself to everybody.

> *"I think that it will end in nothing, Socrates, and that you will win your case, and I will win my own."*

Tell me, Euthyphro, what is your lawsuit? Are you the plaintiff or the defendant?

> *"I am the plaintiff. You will think me mad, Socrates, when I tell you that I am bringing my own father to trial."*

Are you serious? What have you accused him of doing?

> *"Of committing manslaughter."*

That's incredible. But it also illustrates how little most people understand of the nature of justice and truth. Only someone who has made great strides in wisdom could see his way to bring his own father to trial.

> *"That is true."*

I suppose the person your father killed was one of your relatives, because if he had been a stranger, you would never have thought of prosecuting your father.

"*I am amused, Socrates, at your making a distinction between one who is a relative and one who is not a relative, since the crime is the same in either case. The real question is whether the killing is justified. If justified, then our duty is to let the matter alone; but if unjustified, then even if the killer lives under the same roof with us and eats at the same table, we must proceed against him.*

"*Now, in fact, what happened was that one of my father's workers got drunk and murdered one of our domestic slaves. My father caught the murderer, tied his hands and feet, threw him into a ditch. Then my father sent someone to Athens to ask the religious interpreters what he should do. Unfortunately, the murderer died before my father could get advice.*

"*Of course, my family are angry with me for prosecuting my father. They say that my father did not intentionally kill the worker. And even if the worker died because of my father's actions, it is fact that the worker was a murderer. Because of that, they feel that I should not take any action, because a son who prosecutes his father is impious and irreverent. This shows, Socrates, how little they know what the gods think about piety and reverence.*"

You mean to say that your knowledge of what constitutes acts that are pious, impious, reverent, and irreverent is so perfect and comprehensive, that supposing the circumstances to be as you state them, you are not afraid that you, too, may be performing an impious or irreverent act by prosecuting your father?

> *"I am quite certain that I have an exact knowledge of these matters."*

In that case, I will be your disciple. Armed with your knowledge, I will be better equipped to challenge Meletus in court. I will ask Meletus if he agrees that you are a great and wise man. If he agrees, then he should approve of my becoming your disciple and drop the indictment. On the other hand, if he disagrees, then he should indict you, my teacher.

> *"I assure you, Socrates, if Meletus tries to indict me, I will destroy his arguments. When I am finished with him, the court will come down hard on him, not me."*

Now I am even more anxious to become your disciple. I'm surprised that no one appears to have noticed you—not even Meletus. Instead, he has indicted me for impiety. Therefore, please tell me the nature of piety and impiety, which you said you know so well. What are they? Is piety the same in every action, and is impiety always the opposite of piety?

"That is correct, Socrates."

But what exactly is piety, and what is impiety?

"Piety is doing as I am doing; that is to say, prosecuting anyone who is guilty of manslaughter, murder, sacrilege, or any similar crime—whether that person is your father or mother makes no difference—and not to prosecute them is impiety.

"I will prove to you the truth of the principle that the impious should be punished. As you know, Zeus is considered to be the best and most righteous of the gods, and yet he punished his own father for wicked acts. But now, when I proceed against my father, people are angry with me. They are obviously inconsistent in their judgment of how the gods act and how I act."

I see. Perhaps you have uncovered one of the reasons why I am being charged with impiety because, to be honest, I cannot accept these old stories about the gods as being sufficient grounds for ethical principles. I much prefer answers based on reason and rational thinking, not myths. For me, truth is attained by reason. Perhaps that is why many people consider me to be a dangerous person. Instead of old stories about the gods, I would rather hear from you a more precise answer, which you have not yet given, my friend, to my question, "What is piety?" When I asked you the first time you replied that it was doing as you are doing, that is, charging your father with manslaughter.

"And that is the truth, Socrates."

No doubt. But are there many other pious acts?

"Of course there are."

Then maybe I failed to make myself clear. I wasn't asking you to give me one or two examples of piety, but to explain the general idea which makes all pious things pious and all impious things impious. Please explain to me the nature of this idea, and then I shall have a standard by which I may measure acts, whether yours or those of anyone else. I shall be able to say that such and such an act is pious, and another act is impious.

"The general idea is this: Piety is that which is dear to the gods, and impiety is that which is hateful to the gods."

Thank you. You have now given me the answer I wanted. Whether what you say is true or not, I cannot yet tell, although I know that you will try your best to explain it clearly to me.

"Of course, Socrates."

Wonderful. Then let's examine the issue in more detail. You said that something that is "*dear to the gods is pious*," and something that is "*hateful to the gods is impious.*" These two are opposites, is that correct?

"Yes."

And you agree that the gods often make enemies among themselves, and they have hatreds and differences of opinion?

"Yes, the stories tell us so."

Can you give me some examples of the differences of opinion that create enemies and hostility among the gods? For example, suppose that you and I, who are clearly not gods, disagree about an arithmetic problem. Do differences of this sort make us enemies? Or do we simply rely on the principles of arithmetic to settle the issue?

"That is what we would do."

Similarly, if we disagreed about the size or weight of something, we could quickly settle the issue by measuring the object or weighing it, using a stipulated standard of measurement.

"Of course."

But the disagreements that cannot be decided this way, the ones that in fact make us angry and enemies, are disagreements over what is just or unjust, good or evil, honorable or dishonorable, are they not?

"Those are the ones."

Do you suppose that the quarrels of the gods are of the same type?

"Probably."

And isn't it true that everyone loves that which he believes is noble and just and good, but hates the opposite of them?

"It is true."

And we know that these kinds of disputes often result in anger, hatred, and war.

"Sad to say, they often do."

So, a thing might be loved by some gods but hated by other gods, including the question of whether something is pious or impious.

"I suppose so."

Now I am confused. When I asked you to give me a general definition of piety you said: *"Piety is that which is dear to the gods, and impiety is that which is hateful to them."* But now it seems that a thing can be loved by some gods and hated by other gods. Is it possible that your action against your father may likely be doing what is dear to one god, say Zeus, but hateful to another god, for example Cronos? And may there be other gods who have similar differences of opinion?

> *"No, Socrates. I believe that all the gods would be agreed as to the propriety of punishing a person who has committed manslaughter; there would be no difference of opinion about that."*

Yes, but only if they all were sure that the person indeed committed manslaughter. But the basic question, at least among mere mortals, is whether or not someone who has been accused is in fact guilty, isn't that correct?

> *"Yes."*

These are exactly the kinds of questions which humans are always arguing about—especially in courts of law. People commit all sorts of crimes, and there is nothing that they will not do or say in their own defense. But do they usually admit their guilt, and yet say that they should not be punished?

> *"No, they usually deny they are guilty."*

So, people do not generally argue about whether or

not criminals should be punished. The argument is really about the question of whether a crime has been committed in the first place, and, if so, who committed it—in other words, what was done and when.

"Yes."

Then perhaps the gods behave the same way. After all, you said that neither humans nor the gods think that an act of injustice should go unpunished. You also agreed that the gods quarrel about which acts are just and which are unjust. In other words, they can disagree whether a particular act is just or unjust. Moreover, you must agree that some of their actions seem impious or unjust to us. That's why I try to apply reason to these questions instead of relying on the authority of the gods, because which god or gods should we appeal to?

"I see your point, Socrates."

Well then, please help me learn the truth. What proof do you have that, in the opinion of all the gods, a person who has committed a murder and who is put in chains, but who dies before the religious interpreters give their advice, dies unjustly? Moreover, that on behalf of the murderer, a son ought to proceed against his father and accuse him of manslaughter. How would you show that all the gods absolutely agree in approving of this action? Prove to me that they do, and I will applaud your wisdom as long as I live.

"It will be a difficult task, but I think I can make the matter clear even to you."

I know that I am not as quick in understanding as the judges in court, those who you are confident will readily accept your proof that your father's action was unjust and hateful to the gods.

"Yes indeed, Socrates—at least if they will listen to me."

They will be sure to listen, if they find you are a good speaker. Now a thought has just occurred to me. Even if you do prove to me that all the gods regarded the death of the murderer as unjust, then how does that help me know anything more of the nature of piety and impiety? In other words, granting that your father's actions might be hateful to the gods, still, piety and impiety are not adequately defined by this example. I am willing to suppose, if you like, that all the gods condemn your father's actions. I will amend the definition to say that what all the gods hate is impious, and what they all love is pious or holy. Shall this be our new definition of piety and impiety?

"Yes. What all the gods love is pious and holy, and the opposite, which they all hate, is impious."

Good. Should we now investigate the truth of this

61

statement, or simply accept the statement on our own authority and that of others?

> *"We should investigate its truth. But I am confident that the statement will stand the test of inquiry."*

We shall know shortly. The first point I need to understand is whether the pious or holy is loved by the gods because it is holy, or whether it is holy because it is loved by the gods?

> *"I'm sorry to say that I don't understand what you mean, Socrates."*

Let's try an analogy. What is your favorite drink?

> *"Wine."*

Why is that your favorite?

> *"Because it is delicious."*

Is it delicious because you like it, or do you like it because it is delicious? Is your liking it the reason that it is delicious?

> *"I think I understand now. I like it because it is delicious. My liking it doesn't make it delicious."*

But what do you say of piety or holiness, Euthyphro?

According to your definition, isn't what is holy loved by all the gods?

"Yes."

Because it is holy?

"Yes."

It is loved because it is holy, not holy because it is loved.

"I agree."

And that which is dear to the gods is loved by them?

"Yes."

But that which is dear to the gods is dear to them because it is loved by them, not loved by them because it is dear to them.

"True."

But now you must see that being "holy" and being "dear to the gods" are quite different from one another. Therefore, when I asked you for the essence of holiness, you offered only an attribute, not the essence—the attribute of being loved by all the gods. But you still have not explained to me the nature of holiness. Therefore, if you please, I will ask you not to hide your treasure, but to tell me what holiness or piety really is, regardless of whether it is dear to the gods or not. And what is impiety?

"Sorry, Socrates, but I am confused again. I thought I understood your point that something is loved because it is holy, but now I'm not sure about how you are using the term 'dear.' Can you please make your point clearer?"

I'll try. Think of something that is dear to you. Was it dear to you before you loved it, or did it become dear to you after you loved it?

"My loving it made it dear to me. I would not say that anything I hate is dear to me. So, yes, something became dear to me because I loved it, not the other way around."

Good. First we agreed that the holy is loved by the gods because it is holy, not the other way around. Now we see that when the holy is loved by the gods, it becomes dear to them. But its becoming dear to the gods is not its essence. The attribute of "being dear to the gods" does not help us understand the true nature of holiness or piety. Likewise, saying that impiety is that which is hated by the gods does not define its nature.

"I really do not know how to express what I mean, Socrates. Somehow our arguments,

on whatever ground we rest them, seem to turn around and walk away from us."

Since these ideas are your own, Euthyphro, you must agree that they themselves show an inclination to be on the move. I would like nothing better than to believe in them and keep them fixed, but until we do we must continue our analysis. We must begin again and ask: *"What is piety?"* That is an inquiry which I shall never be weary of pursuing. I hope that you are not angry with me. Please apply your great knowledge and firm mind to this problem, and help me understand the truth. I am confident that, if anyone knows, you are the one. Therefore, I must detain you until you teach me the truth. I am certain that, if you had not known the true nature of piety and impiety, then you would never have charged your father with manslaughter. You would not have run such a risk of doing wrong in the sight of the gods, and you would have had too much respect for the opinions of men. Therefore, I am sure that you know the nature of piety and impiety. Speak out—do not hide your knowledge.

"I have told you already, Socrates, that for you to learn all these things accurately will be tiresome. But perhaps this will have to wait for another time. I am in a hurry and must go now."

You leave me in despair, Euthyphro. I was hoping that you would instruct me in the nature of piety and impiety, so I might clear myself of Meletus and his indictment. I would tell him that I had been enlightened by Euthyphro, and that now I am about to lead a better life. Instead, our conversation has ended without a firm resolution. So long, Euthyphro, until we meet again.

I was sorry to see him go. There was much more for us to discuss. But perhaps the necessity of long-term rational examination explains why few people are willing to follow that path. Like Euthyphro, they prefer quick answers. But an answer without knowledge of why it is correct is not satisfying, and that fact explains why many people go from one quick answer to another. This also explains why some beliefs based solely on myth or authority are ultimately unsatisfactory. The authorities demand unquestioned faith and strict obedience, and their quick condemnation of any doubt stifles rational thought and reasoned examination. Thus, they relinquish any honest pursuit of knowledge because knowledge can happen only through reason and serious examination.

I tried to show Euthyphro that although he had a strong belief that his actions against his father were justified, if his belief could not withstand reasonable analysis, but led instead to obvious contradictions, then it rested on a faulty foundation. I tried to show him that since his actions are the end point of the beliefs and rules that he follows, the important thing is to see what effects are realized in the real world, what practical consequences result from following those beliefs and rules.

With that said, let's return to your request asking me to clarify what I mean by a "a just person" and "justice." If, in the past, I failed to explain it in words, I have tried to do so in my actions. If a person's actions are a direct window to his character, then tell me, Hippias, do you not think that an action is worth more as evidence than a word?

> *"It is worth far more. Many a man with justice and right on his lips commits injustice and wrong, but no doer of right ever commits injustice."*

Then I ask if you have ever seen or heard of me bearing false witness, or spreading malicious information, or stirring up strife among friends, or causing political dissension in the city, or committing any other unjust and wrongful act?

> *"No, I cannot say that I have."*

And do you not regard it as right and just to abstain from doing wrong?

> *"Socrates, are you defining 'a just person' by reference not to what a person does, but what he does not do?"*

I firmly believe that the refusal to do wrong is a sufficient warrant of righteousness and justice. But if you do not agree, then see if this pleases you better: I assert that what is "lawful" is "just and righteous."

"Do you mean to assert that 'lawful' and 'just' are synonymous terms?"

I do.

"But I am still at a loss to understand exactly what you mean by 'lawful' and 'just.' Please clarify this for me."

You understand what is meant by the laws of a city or state?

"Of course."

What do you take them to be?

"They are the enactments drawn up by the citizens or representatives of a state in agreement as to what things should be done or left undone."

Then I presume that a member of a state who regulates his life in accordance with these enactments will be law-abiding, but the transgressor of the same will be lawless.

"That follows."

And I also presume that a law-abiding citizen will do what is just and right, but a lawless citizen will do what is unjust and wrong.

"I agree."

And he who does what is just is just, and he who does what is unjust is unjust.

"Of course."

It would appear, then, that the law-abiding citizen is just, and the lawless citizen is unjust.

"But isn't it true, Socrates, that the people who make the laws often reject or change them?"

That is also true of war, Hippias. People often go to war, but then seek peace.

"True."

If that is so, then what would be the difference between diminishing the value of obeying existing laws because laws might be repealed eventually, and diminishing the value of good discipline in war because peace will one day be made? But perhaps you object to enthusiasm displayed in defense of one's country in war?

"No, I do not."

Indeed, of all the blessings which a state may enjoy, none stands higher than the blessing of unanimity. The citizens should be bound together by an oath of agreement. Not, of course, as implying that citizens shall all agree as to the best poet or musician, or to seek the same pleasures, but simply that they shall pay obedience to the laws.

And if we turn to private life, what better protection can a person have than obedience to the laws? This should be the safeguard against penalties and the guarantee of honors at the hands of the community. It should provide a path through the maze of the law courts. It is to the law-abiding citizen that others will turn in confidence when seeking a guardian of their money, or the safety of their children.

And now, Hippias, I have done my part in demonstrating that the "lawful" and "law-observant" are synonymous with the "upright" and the "just." If you hold a contrary view, please instruct us.

"It seems, Socrates, that you see the terms 'just' and 'lawful' as being two sides of the same coin."

Yes, and I try to provide concrete examples to illustrate in practical terms what I mean. But perhaps my intent to hit a target is not always realized. Sometimes our analysis takes us down a path searching for strict definitions that have a universal application. But we can get lost because the path ends without a final resolution, and we don't have the tools needed to cut our way through the dense forest. At those times it helps to rest and survey where we have been, to look around and place markers to guide us on our next search. Grounding our abstract thoughts in concrete examples can provide some of the tools to help us resume our search. Therefore, we can use our actions themselves to illustrate practical real-world effects of "just" and "unjust." We should strive to mesh reason with human actions and behaviors to see not only the logical consequences, but the actual outcomes of our actions. By this method, we can observe if our actions promote the best outcomes and happiness among people and, if so, then they are just and lawful, and we become virtuous and wise.

"But why do people change the laws so often, Socrates?"

History shows us that laws and human actions are constantly affecting each other. Laws get changed when we see that certain unwanted actions and behaviors escape the law's net. This can occur when a law is so poorly written that vagueness leads to unintended consequences, or when a law contains a logical error. Likewise, actions or behaviors that lead to unwanted social ills cause new laws to be written to prohibit such behavior. In order for a society to remain healthy, it has to observe the ongoing relationship between laws and behaviors, so it can make mutual adjustments between laws and accepted behaviors.

In addition, laws can be challenged; but our challenges must take place peacefully. If we believe a law is unjust, then we should peacefully disobey it, but we must be willing to accept the wrath of some members of society who see such behavior as threatening to society. If our peaceful disobedience has a just foundation, then there is hope that an unjust law will eventually be overturned.

Perhaps, then, we can use this as a guide to begin understanding the dynamic relationships between justice, virtue, knowledge, and wisdom in that they each need to be connected to actions or behaviors— the concreteness of the world—where the outcomes or effects of our actions can be observed.

"But, Socrates, you agree that laws can be twisted or perverted by unscrupulous people. What can we do to prevent this?"

That is why I maintain that each person must strive to achieve wisdom, virtue, and knowledge. And since the laws by themselves are not sufficient to teach people these things, each of us needs patience and dedication to help with individual training, teaching, and education in which open, free, and honest discussion and examination can take place through the application of reason in the pursuit of truth. ≈ ≈ ≈

≈ ≈ ≈ It is good to see you again, Euthydemus. Please correct me if I am wrong, but I recall you saying that your "natural ability" is enough to qualify you as meeting the requisite requirements to be a statesman. If the state encounters some problem, you are confident that you can provide the solution. Further, you always make sure to emphasize to your listeners that you have not learned anything from anybody. I tried to engage you on these topics many times, but you were reluctant. I even told you that I could imagine you talking to a group of senators, so I made up the following speech for you: *"Citizens of Athens, I have never at any time learned anything from anybody; nor, if I have ever heard of anyone as being an able statesman, well versed in speech and capable of action, have I sought to meet him. I have not tried to provide myself with a teacher from amongst those who have knowledge. On the contrary, I have persistently avoided the faintest suspicion of so doing. Anything that occurs to me by the light of nature I shall be glad to place at your disposal."*

But even after my putting those words in your mouth, you still refused to engage in dialogue. I now offer the following criticism of the hypothetical speech, hoping to prompt a response. My friends, suppose Euthydemus sought the office of state physician, and he said, *"Citizens of Athens, I have never sought the teaching of any physician. In fact, I have been against the notion of having to study medicine at all. If you will be so good as to confer on me this post, I promise I will do my best to acquire skill by experimenting on you."*

Still no response from you, Euthydemus? Never mind. In the meantime, let me say that it is not surprising that people anxious to learn to play the flute, or to become proficient in any skill, are not content to work in private, but they also seek out the most esteemed teachers. But, ironically, many who aspire to become politicians and statesmen cannot see why they shouldn't be able to do all that politics demands at a moment's notice, by sheer inspiration, without any preliminary preparation whatsoever. And yet it seems to me that becoming an honest and effective politician is more difficult than becoming a good flute player since the politician's acts can lead to serious consequences to society. Although there seems to be no lack of people seeking political office, it also appears that few have devoted the time necessary to become great leaders. Tell me, Euthydemus, is it really true that you have collected several works of the classical authors and philosophers?

> *"Quite true, Socrates, and I mean to go on collecting until I have all the great books I can possibly acquire."*

I admire you for wishing to have treasures of wisdom rather than of gold and silver, which shows that you do not believe gold and silver to be the means of making us better, but the thoughts of the wise enrich us with virtue and wisdom. And what is it in which you desire to excel, Euthydemus, that makes you collect books? Have you turned your back on politics? Perhaps now you want to be a great physician? If so, then the prescriptions of the Pharmacopoeia would form a large library by themselves.

"No, I do not wish to be a physician."

Then do you wish to be an architect? That too implies a person having extensive knowledge and sound judgment.

"I have no such ambition."

Do you wish to be a mathematician?

"No, not a mathematician."

Then do you wish to be an astronomer? Or a reciter of epic poems? I am told you have the entire works of Homer.

"No, not an astronomer. And, heaven forbid, not a reciter of epic poems, since that lot may achieve perfection in the art of reciting epic poetry, but they are apt to be simpletons themselves."

Can it be, Euthydemus, that you still aspire to that excellence through which men become statesmen and administrators, fit to rule and benefactors to the rest of the world and themselves?

"Yes, that is the excellence I desire beyond measure."

Ah, then you have indeed selected as the object of your ambition the noblest of virtues and the greatest of the arts. But have you considered whether it is possible to excel in these matters without being just and upright?

"I have considered that, Socrates, and I claim that without justice and uprightness it is impossible to be a good citizen."

No doubt you have accomplished that initial step?

"I think I could hold my own against all comers as an upright person."

And do upright people have distinctive and appropriate work like those of carpenters or shoemakers?

"To be sure they have."

And as the carpenter is able to exhibit his work and products, the righteous man should be able to expound and set forth his, should he not?

"I see you are afraid that I cannot expound the works of righteousness. Why, of course I can, and the works of unrighteousness into the bargain, since there are many of that sort within easy reach of eye and ear every day."

Shall we then write the letter "R" on this side of the ledger, and on the other side the letter "U"? And then anything that appears to us to be the product of righteousness and justice we will place under the R account, and anything which appears to be the product of unrighteousness and injustice under the U account?

"By all means do so, if you think that it will assist matters."

To begin, then, lying exists among humans, even among friends, does it not?

"Of course, no one could deny that."

To which side of the account shall we place it?

"Clearly on the side of unrighteousness and injustice."

Deceit too is quite common, again, even among friends?

"Yes."

To which side shall we place deceit?

"On the U side."

And we cannot allow any of these to be on the R side of the account, to the side of right and justice, can we, Euthydemus?

"It would be monstrous."

Very good. But suppose a man is elected general, and he succeeds in enslaving an unjust, wicked, and hostile state. Are we to say that he is doing wrong?

"By no means."

Suppose he deceives his foes while at war with them.

"That would be all fair and right also. But when you began, Socrates, I thought you were limiting the questions to the case of friends."

To get a full picture of these topics we must expand our view. Now, given your answers to the previous questions, some things that we originally set down on the U side will now have to be placed to the R side.

"It appears so."

Very well then, let us so place them. And please, let us make a new definition: That while it is right to do such things to a foe, it is wrong to do them to a friend, for in dealing with our friends we must always be as straightforward as possible.

"I quite agree."

So far, so good. But if a general, seeing his troops demoralized, were to invent a tale to the effect that reinforcements were coming, and by means of this false statement should revive the courage of his men, to which of the two accounts shall we place that act of fraud?

"On the side of right, to my thinking."

Now suppose a mother chanced to have a child in need of medicine, which the child refused to take; and suppose the mother, by an act of deceit, administers it under the guise of something pleasant to eat, and by using that lie restores the child to health. To which account shall we set down this fraud?

"In my judgment, it too should be placed in the R account."

But now suppose you have a friend who is so terribly depressed that you are afraid he will kill himself. And suppose you rob him of his knife. To which side ought we to set the theft?

> *"That too must surely be placed on the R side of the ledger."*

So, I understand you to say that the straightforward course of action is not always to be pursued, even when dealing with friends?

> *"Heaven forbid! If you will allow me, I rescind my former statement."*

Allow you? Of course you may, anything rather than make a false entry on our list. But there is another point we need to investigate. Let us take the case of deceiving a friend to his detriment. Which would be the more wrongful act: to deceive intentionally or unintentionally?

> *"Really, Socrates, I have ceased to believe in my own answers, for all my former admissions and conceptions seem to me other than I first supposed them. Still, if I may hazard one more opinion, the intentional deceiver, I should say, is worse than the unintentional."*

And is it your opinion that there is a knowledge of right and justice as there is of spelling and grammar?

> *"That is my opinion."*

And who would you say was the better speller—one who intentionally misspells, or one who does so unintentionally?

> *"The one who does so intentionally because he can spell and read correctly whenever he chooses."*

Then the voluntary misspeller is likely a literate person, but the involuntary offender may be merely illiterate?

> *"True. I do not see how to escape from that conclusion."*

And which of the two knows what is right—the one who intentionally lies and deceives, or the one who lies and deceives unintentionally?

> *"Clearly, it is the intentional and conscious liar."*

Well then, your position comes to this: On the one hand, the person who has the knowledge of spelling is more learned than one who has no such knowledge.

> *"Yes."*

And someone who has knowledge of things right and just is more righteous than someone who lacks that knowledge.

"I suppose it is true, but for the life of me I cannot make sense of my own statements."

Look at it like this. Suppose someone is anxious to speak the truth, but he is never able to hold the same thoughts about a thing for two minutes. First he says: *"The road is toward the east,"* and then he says, *"No, it's toward the west."* On another occasion, when he adds a column of figures, first he makes this the sum, and then he makes it something else. What do you think of such a person?

"Heaven help us! Clearly he does not know what he thought he knew."

If someone is simply confused, or worse, if he contradicts himself unwittingly, then can we say that he is in a state of ignorance, that he lacks the appropriate knowledge or wisdom in a given situation?

"Yes."

For instance, a person may be ignorant of medicine, or carpentry, or shoemaking, or farming, or any number of things.

"Yes."

And would you say that many people are ignorant of what justice means?

82

"It is quite likely. I'm sorry to say, Socrates, that I did flatter myself that I was a student of philosophy, and on the right road to understanding everything essential to one who makes justice and goodness his pursuit. So now you may well imagine my despair when, for all my effort, I cannot even answer the questions put to me about what a person should know."

Do not despair, Euthydemus. Tell me, have you ever been to The Temple of Apollo at Delphi?

"Yes, twice."

And did you notice the inscription on the temple: "Know Thyself."

"I did."

And did you possibly pay no regard to the inscription? Or did you think about it and try to discover who and what you were?

"I can honesty say I did not. And now I see that if I did not know even myself, what in the world did I know?"

Can someone know himself who knows his own name and nothing more? Or must he not rather set to work precisely like a purchaser of a horse, who does not think that he has got the knowledge he requires until he has discovered whether the horse is strong or weak, or quick or slow, or whatever the intended use is to be? Likewise, we must investigate our own nature and learn to know our own capacities. And this too is clear: That through self-knowledge we attain well-being; but through ignorance of ourselves we court trouble. The person who knows himself knows what is beneficial to himself; he discerns the limits of his powers, and by doing what he knows, he provides himself with what he needs. And by not trying to apply his ignorance to a situation, he avoids mistakes and thereby mishaps. In contrast, he who does not know himself and is mistaken as to his own abilities, puts himself and others in jeopardy. What is true of individuals is true also of communities.

> *"Rest assured, Socrates, that I fully agree with you. The precept 'Know Thyself' cannot be too highly valued. But what is the starting-point of self-examination? I look to you for an explanation, if you would kindly give one."*

I presume you know quite well the distinction between good and bad things?

> *"Why, yes, to be sure."*

Very well. Please tell me what you think.

"That is, fortunately for me, not difficult. First of all, health in itself I hold to be a good, and disease in itself an evil; but the sources of either of those, for example, meat, drinks, and habits of life, I regard as good or evil according as they contribute either to health or to disease."

A fine answer. But are health or disease, when they prove to be a source of good, themselves good, and when a source of evil, themselves evil?

"But Socrates, how can health be a source of evil, or disease a source of good?"

In the event, for instance, of some battle, where those who, owing to their health and strength, take part and are killed, while those who were too ill or weak to fight survive.

"I see. But you must admit that there are some advantages to be had from strength and lost through weakness."

Yes, but ought we to regard those things which at one moment benefit and at another moment injure us in any strict sense good rather than evil?

"Not according to that line of argument. But you must admit that wisdom is always good, since there is nothing which, or in

which, a wise person would not do better than a fool."

Have you heard of Daedalus, and how he was seized by Minos on account of his wisdom, and forced to be his slave, and robbed of country and freedom at one fell swoop? And how, while endeavoring to make his escape with his son, he caused the boy's death without bringing about his own salvation, and instead was carried off and again enslaved?

"Yes, I know the story."

Have you heard of the woes of Palamedes, how for his wisdom's sake Odysseus envied him and slew him?

"That, too, I know."

And how many do you suppose have been condemned to death on account of their wisdom?

"Then how about prosperity or well-being? Surely, those must be a blessing, Socrates."

It might be so, if it chanced not to be in itself a compound of other questionable blessings.

"And which among the components of happiness and well-being can possibly be questionable?"

None, unless of course we are to include among these components beauty, or strength, or wealth, or reputation, or anything else of that kind.

> *"Of course we must include them, for what would happiness be without them?"*

Yes, but then we shall be including the commonest sources of mischief which befall mankind. How many admirers are driven to distraction by the sight of beauty in its bloom? How many, tempted by their strength to do deeds beyond their power, are involved in tragedies? How many, rendered weak by their wealth, have been plotted against and destroyed? How many, through fame and political power, have suffered a world of woe?

> *"If I am not even right in praising happiness, then I must confess I know little."*

Perhaps these are simply matters which through excessive confidence in your knowledge of them, you have failed to examine thoroughly. But since the state, which you are preparing yourself to direct, is democratically constituted, of course you know what constitutes a democracy.

> *"I hope so."*

Well, now, is it possible to know what a democratic state is without knowing who the people are?

"No."

And who are the people?

"The poor and the rich citizens."

Who are the poor and rich citizens?

"By poor I mean those who have not enough to pay for their necessities, and by rich those who have more than sufficient means for all their needs."

Have you noticed that some who have a mere pittance find this sufficient, and actually succeed in getting a surplus out of it; while others do not find a large fortune quite large enough?

"I have, and I thank you for the reminder. I have heard of crowned heads and despotic rulers being driven by desire for more power and wealth who caused horrible suffering on innocent people. But now I think it is time for me to keep silent. I have lots to think about, Socrates."

Fear not, Euthydemus. Although you are young, you already understand that what you seek takes patience and the willingness to engage in conversation. Apply your obvious talents to a dedicated self-examination, and continue to seek out differing opinions. Eagerly engage yourself in reasoned argumentation with people who are not afraid to put their arguments to the test, and you will benefit immensely from those experiences. ≈≈≈

≈ ≈ ≈ Pericles, I'm glad you joined us. We just enjoyed a wonderful discussion about the necessary requirements to be a good politician. And since you are the son of a great statesman, I expect great improvement in our military affairs when you become minister of war.

> *"Although I hope that your wish is fulfilled, I'm not completely confident that it will come to pass."*

Shall we consider the arguments for and against the possibility?

> *"Yes, I welcome the opportunity."*

It seems to me that the state was never more disposed, never so ripe for a really good leader, as it is today. If boldness is the parent of carelessness, laxity, and insubordination, then it seems that fear can make people more disposed to careful decisions, attentiveness, and obedience. A proof of which you may observe in the behavior of people on ships. In seasons of calm weather when there is nothing to fear, disorder sometimes occurs; but as soon as there is apprehension of a storm, or an enemy in sight, the scene changes; not only is each word of command obeyed, but there is a hush of silent expectation; the mariners wait to catch the next signal like an orchestra with eyes upon the leader.

"I agree. As you say, now is the time for us to rekindle a desire in the people to obey commands and the law. But we must also explain how we are to rekindle those old fires, the passionate longing for valor, for the glory and the wellbeing of the days of old."

Since our objective should be to set their sights on virtue, we must prove to them that virtue is a time-honored heritage.

"How do we begin?"

By reminding them of a fact already registered in their minds: That the oldest of our ancestors whose names are known to us were also the bravest of heroes. Therefore, amidst the many changes in society, brave people maintained their virtue, and looked to the laws and courts to maintain justice.

"But given this heritage, Socrates, what caused our city to decline?"

We became victims of our own success. We were like a once great athlete whose easy success betrayed him into laziness until he eventually was overtaken by those more dedicated to training. So we Athenians, at the height of our powers, have neglected ourselves, and over time have become weak.

> *"What should we do now to recover our former virtues?"*

There is no mystery about that. We can either rediscover the institutions of our past, applying them to the regulation of our lives with something of their precision, or we can imitate those who today display virtuous behavior, in which case, if we live up to the standard of these models, we may hope to approach their excellence.

> *"Perhaps I am too pessimistic, Socrates. It seems to me that the spirit of virtue and bravery has taken wings and left our city. For instance, many people today neglect their elders, so acts of reverence are diminishing. In addition, not only do many people neglect to take the care of their bodies through exercise and good diet, these same people ridicule those who spend the time needed to stay healthy. Many of our fellow citizens seem to take pride in despising the knowledge of experts and anyone with authority. How can we again be united as a people?*

"We who, instead of combining to promote common interests, delight in demeaning each other's characters and envying one another. We are torn by dissension and are caught in a maze of litigation, and prefer to make capital out of our neighbor's difficulties rather than to render natural assistance. We treat our national interests no better than if they were the concerns of some foreign state. We make them bones of contention to wrangle over, and rejoice in nothing so much as in possessing the means and ability to indulge these tastes. From this hotbed is engendered in the state a spirit of blind folly and cowardice, and in the hearts of the citizens spreads a tangle of hatred and mutual hostility which, as I often shudder to think, will some day cause some disaster to befall the state greater than it can bear."

That is quite an indictment, Pericles. And although I agree with you on many points, I ask you not to conclude that Athens has become so smitten with depravity that it is incurable. Athens is made of people, and people can, and do, become virtuous when given the right guidance. Consider the military as one example. You know that many members still observe discipline. In athletics, many eagerly follow the advice of their instructors. And we have many fine choruses, actors, playwrights, merchants, and farmers. So the seeds of virtue and wisdom are still alive in Athens, they just need to be sown more widely.

> *"That's the wonder of it, Socrates. To think that all those people continue to lead good and honest lives in such trying times is heartening. But how do we instill these characteristics in others? Or is it just by chance that these good people rise up?"*

Are there some councils composed of citizens of noble character?

> *"Yes, there are."*

And do you also admit that there are some similar bodies, judicial or executive, trying cases or transacting other business with great honor, strict legality, high dignity, and impartial justice?

> *"Yes."*

Then we ought not to despair as though all sense of orderliness and good discipline has died out of our country.

> *"But I still hold that in military service where temperance, orderliness, and good discipline are needed, these essentials receive scant attention by those in charge."*

May it not perhaps be that they are being lead by those who have the least knowledge? No one should ever dream of leading if that person lacks the requisite knowledge. But it is a sad fact that today many military leaders got their positions through influence, not through knowledge. I know that you are not one of them. I believe you could give a clear account of your schooling in strategy. No doubt you have been influenced by your father's "rules for generalship," which you have carefully preserved, besides having collected many others from which it is possible to gain knowledge which would be useful to a future general. I feel sure you are deeply concerned to overcome ignorance of anything that might be useful to you in so high an office. And if you detect in yourself any ignorance, you will not hesitate to turn to those who have knowledge in these matters to exchange your ignorance for their knowledge and to secure their help.

"I am not so blind, Socrates, as to imagine you say these words under the idea that I am truly so careful in these matters; but rather your object is to teach me that the would-be general must make such things his care. I admit in any case all you say."

If these suggestions are agreeable, then try your best to realize them. If you can carry out a portion of them, then it will be an honor to yourself and a blessing to the state. If your honest effort happens to fail at any point, there will be no damage done to the city, or discredit to yourself.

> *"Socrates, you said earlier that you consider my father to be a great statesman, so you must know the qualities necessary to be a good politician. If you don't mind, I would like to know why you never entered politics. I believe that you would have inspired others to follow your example."*

I thought my efforts would be served best by engaging people one-on-one in order to have deep discussions about character and justice, instead of merely offering fragile aphorisms that are unlikely to take root. In this way, I felt I could contribute to making better citizens, some of whom might become politicians, rather to practice politics myself.

We can bring about change if we deter others from clinging to false beliefs, weak arguments, and bad behavior, and by so doing lay a foundation for the pursuit of virtue. It is far better to struggle along a road that leads to becoming a good person, than to find a quick avenue to becoming someone merely thought to be good. Someone who gets money or goods out of another person by fraud or flattery harms that person. But of all imposters, he surely is the biggest who can delude enough people into thinking that he is fit to lead the state, when all the while he is a worthless creature.

Many people, especially politicians and those who have achieved some measure of fame, believe they are able to change the behavior of large numbers of society. But history shows that those kinds of changes are temporary because they are superficial. They are the result of a cult of personality in which the ideas or beliefs are not ingrained in the followers, but instead are a temporary mimic response that soon fades away upon the advent of a new popular cult. The opposite of this is when a society changes because individuals change themselves. Lasting change can come only from an internal process whereby the character is formed. This works by a careful reasoning process—a step-by-step self-examination of a person's beliefs. This is not a quick process; it requires dedication and an open mind that is willing to work through difficult problems. It can be facilitated by open dialogue with others who are also seeking answers, who are driven by a rigorous application of reasoning and argument. Since this slow process can substantially change a person, its effects are long-lasting. This is why I engage people one-on-one, and it explains why I never entered politics or gave speeches to the masses. A speech is not a dialogue. It has one direction, talking at a person instead of talking with a person. Self-examination and dialogues with others are the ways to lasting individual character change; thus, it can affect profound changes in society.

We must be honest with ourselves and others when we seek truth and wisdom. Of course, a political speech, or the opinion of a famous person can be attractive and sound persuasive, but accepting it at face value without any examination of its foundation absolves the listeners of the responsibility to think for themselves. The acceptance is fleeting because it is taken in without a rational foundation that is based on rigorous and honest examination. Inevitably, as soon as the politician or famous person is exposed as shallow or corrupt, the followers abandon him and move on to the next personality. In contrast, those who develop wisdom and virtue through clear reasoning thereby acquire a depth of knowledge that secures their acting justly and ethically. Each of us spends a great deal of time thinking about the problems of life, and in those times we think about practical applications of justice, virtue, honesty, and knowledge. If we are fortunate, we will have relatives or friends to share our thoughts, discuss our problems, and possibly find solutions. We tend to forget that the daily actions of every citizen are important, and the cumulative actions of all citizens form the character of a society.

Our needs are practical; to live, to interact safely with each other, to not have to worry about injustice, to help each other, among many other things. Our actions determine what happens to ourselves and others. Our actions paint a picture of our character. I can see who I am by looking at what I did. My character is the sum of my past actions. ≈ ≈ ≈

≈ ≈ ≈ We should avoid believing that we are absolutely certain, because that often leads to arrogance and fanaticism. It is better to be a fearless questioner, as I tried to show those engaged in free-wheeling discussions. Suppose you had two sorts of things, one which presents no clue as to what it is for, and the other which has some obviously useful purpose. Which would you judge to be the result of chance, which of design, Aristodemus?

"Clearly that which is produced for some useful end must be the work of design."

Then is it likely that humans were made for some useful end? Could it be that all our senses—eyes to behold the visible word, ears to catch the intonations of sound, a nose to respond to scents, a tongue to not only perceive sweet or pungent things, but allow for the possibility of forming words, thoughts and arguments—are designed for a purpose or function? And speaking of our sense of smell, some people have argued that since matter passing out of the body is unpleasant, the position on our body of the avenue of escape is such that the hind-ward direction releases unpleasant odors away from the nose. I ask you, when you see all these things constructed with such foresight, do you believe they are the products of intelligence or chance?

"Viewed in this light they seem to be the handiwork of some wise designer, full of love for all living things."

Then what shall we say of this passion implanted in man to beget offspring, and in the offspring itself, once born, this deep desire of life and fear of death?

"No doubt these look like the contrivances of someone who deliberately planned the existence of living creatures."

And do you sometimes feel that you have a spark of wisdom?

"Ask your questions, and I will try to answer."

I am happy to hear that. But notice that when considering the most important questions that continually puzzle us, we often imagine that our tiny grasp of the universe is up to the task of formulating definite answers. We know that we observe only a tiny fragment of the earth, a little drop of the vast oceans and of the other elements. But how this really came about, and what our place in the great scheme of things actually comes to, it seems, rests on a fragile foundation that we ourselves have created.

"It may be, for my eyes fail to see the master agents of these, as one sees the fabricators of things produced on earth."

No more do you see your own soul, which is the master agent of your body; so that, as far as things go, you may maintain, if you like, that you do nothing with intelligence, but everything by chance.

But suppose we are afraid of seeking truth by ourselves, so we instead go to those we call "authorities." Now we must separate two types of authority. The first are those who deal with practical and concrete problems, such as carpentry, medicine, shipbuilding, farming, horse training, to mention only a few. The "right actions" of those engaged in these activities involve what we can call the "proper work or function" of such actions. Successful practitioners earn their reputations by a history of successful outcomes.

> *"But Socrates, you cannot compare these kind of experts with the authorities that have to deal with more complex ideas, such as distinguishing a just from an unjust act, of determining who is pious and who is impious. Here myth or religious authorities are our best guides."*

This is the second kind of authority that I alluded to earlier, and which I will now discuss. It is my position that the two types are not that different. The second type also involve themselves with concrete human actions, so they are similar to the experts in practical arts. Both types of authorities deal with actions that involve ourselves—our characters—and the consequences that our actions have on others. Individual actions ripple through society because a society is made of individuals and their actions. The same is true for the practical authorities, such as shipbuilding. The shipbuilders must endeavor to learn as much as possible so they are up to the task; they must strive for self-improvement, and they should display virtuous behavior. When we observe their success in creating well-constructed ships, or when we observe their willingness and ability to teach others, we see the outward consequences of their actions.

Therefore, I hold that we should look at the results of our actions in all that we do. We should consider what we hope to achieve by our behavior and observe what consequences actually occur. I need to examine what my intentions are, what purpose or function that I wish to bring about by my actions in my constant and daily practical matters when I interact with others. This is the bread and butter of my existence. And if I was designed by some power that I shall never know, or if I exist only by chance, my actions let me know immediately what I am. In this manner I can see my true character, and, if I have the courage, try to adjust my actions toward the character I want to become. It comes to this: Every honest person should look upon self-control as the cornerstone of virtue that forms the basis of our actions. ≈ ≈ ≈

≈ ≈ ≈ Is anyone here willing to explain the nature of piety? I ask because I once had a stimulating discussion with Euthyphro which, unfortunately, was interrupted before we could come to a resolution.

"Piety is something excellent, no doubt."

A fine start, thank you. Now can you tell me what constitutes a pious person?

"A person who honors the gods."

And is it allowable to honor the gods in any mode or fashion one likes?

"No, there are laws that we must follow."

Then someone who knows these laws will know how to honor the gods?

"I think so."

And those who know how they must honor the gods also know that they should not do so except in the manner which follows this knowledge. Is that correct?

"It is."

And does anyone honor the gods in a way that goes against that knowledge?

"I think not."

So it comes to this: Someone who knows what the laws require in reference to the gods will honor the gods in the lawful way.

"Yes."

But now, those who honor lawfully honor as they should.

"I see no alternative."

And those who honor as they should are pious?

"Yes."

It appears, then, that those who know what the law requires with respect to the gods will correctly be defined as pious, and that is our definition?

"So it appears to me, at any rate."

But now, with regard to human beings, is it allowable to deal with other people in any way one pleases?

"No. With regard to other people, a law-abiding person is one who knows what things are lawful concerning others and acts accordingly in his dealings with other people."

Then those who deal with one another in this way deal with each other as they should.

"Obviously."

And those who deal with one another as they should, deal well and nobly. And those who deal well and nobly by mankind are well-doers in respect of human affairs.

"Yes."

I presume that those who obey the laws do what is right and just?

"Without a doubt."

And what do we mean by right and just?

"What the laws ordain."

It seems to follow that those who do what the laws ordain do what is right and just, and what they should.

"I see no alternative."

Let's see what we have uncovered. Those who know what the law demands do what is right and just, and those who do what is right and just are righteous and just. In other words, knowing leads to doing, and doing leads to righteousness and justice. This is an important link between ideas.

"I agree."

And what shall we say about the nature of wisdom? Tell me, does it seem to you that the wise are wise in what they know, or are there any who are wise in what they don't know?

"Clearly they are wise in what they know, for how could anyone have wisdom of something that he does not know?"

In fact, then, the wise are wise in knowledge. Given this, it seems to follow that wisdom and knowledge are really the same thing—if you have one, then you automatically have the other.

"So it appears to me."

Is it possible for someone to know everything?

"I don't think that is possible."

Then it would be impossible for someone to be all-wise.

"Quite impossible."

The wisdom of each of us is limited to our particular knowledge; each is wise only in what he actually knows.

"That is my opinion."

Now, concerning that which we call "the good," does it seem to you that the same thing is equally advantageous to everyone?

"No, I should say not."

Would you say that a thing which is beneficial to one person is sometimes hurtful to another?

"I imagine that can be the case."

And is there anything else good except that which is beneficial?

"Nothing else."

Then it follows that something beneficial is good relative to him to whom it is beneficial?

"That is how it appears to me."

May the same be said of "beauty"? Can we speak of a thing as beautiful in any other way than in relative terms? Or can you name any beautiful thing, whatever it might be, which you know of as universally beautiful?

"I confess I do not know of any such myself."

Perhaps we can capture it this way: To turn a thing to its proper use is to apply it beautifully.

"That sounds promising."

To continue this line of thought we need to show concrete instances, practical cases where we feel confident that our ideas are progressing in the right direction. Perhaps determining how some complex ideas can be illustrated through real-life situations may eventually lead to a greater universal understanding of the most important concepts. And I hope to be able to speak with you about this in the future, after we have individually thought about these things for a while. ≈ ≈ ≈

≈ ≈ ≈ Critobulus, you have a reputation for practical knowledge. I once heard you claim that farming is partly a hand-me-down set of procedures, and partly a willingness and ability to react and improvise when the future doesn't match our intended plans. Also, a farmer can always seek help from those more experienced in farming if problems arise. And if you want to grow something new, you can ask someone who has tried growing it to see what they learned from the experience. Therefore, farming is an individual and collective body of knowledge. I would like to ask you if a person who practices farming is like those who practice medicine, carpentry, shipbuilding, metal-working, and so forth;

in other words, is it a particular knowledge or science?

"Yes it is."

Since we can state the proper work or function of each of the practices just named—or "arts," if we may call them by that name—can we likewise state the proper work and function of farming?

"At the very least, a good farmer must be able to manage his own estate well."

Suppose, for some reason, the farmer is called away. The farmer then needs to hire someone to manage the farm as skillfully as he would. Since a person who is skilled in carpentry can work as well for another as for himself, this ought to be equally true of a good farmer.

"Assuredly."

Then there is no reason why someone skilled in this art, even if he does not happen to have wealth of his own, should not be paid for managing someone else's farm?

"None at all. He would be entitled to earn a large salary, especially if, after paying the necessary expenses of the estate entrusted to him, he can create a surplus and improve the property."

So you believe that wealth consists of things which benefit us?

"Yes."

And a thing can be either beneficial or not beneficial, depending on whether a person knows or does not know how to use it. For instance, a flute may be beneficial to someone who is sufficiently skilled to play it, but the same instrument is no better than the stones we tread under our feet to someone who is not skilled, unless he chose to sell it.

> *"That is precisely the conclusion we should come to. To a person ignorant of its use, a flute can be sold, but if it is not sold, then it has no value for that person. Observe how smoothly and consistently the argument proceeds, since it is admitted that things which benefit us are wealth. The unsold flute in question is not wealth, being good for nothing; to become wealth it must be sold."*

Presuming the owner knows how to sell it. Supposing he were to sell it for something which he does not know how to use; then the mere selling will not transform it into anything beneficial, according to your argument.

"But he may sell it for money. Are you saying, Socrates, that money itself in the pockets of a person who does not know how to use it is not wealth?"

That depends on whether you agree to the truth of the following proposition: Wealth is that, and that only, whereby a person may be benefited.

"I agree."

Then let money be banished to the remote corners of the earth rather than be reckoned as wealth. But now, what shall we say of friends?

"Friends are indisputably wealth, and in a deeper sense than mere possessions, if, as may be supposed, they are likely to prove of more benefit to us than wealth of cattle."

What a strange thing to say—that friends have a market value. If we judge our friends by some measure of market value, then shouldn't we examine ourselves to see what we are worth to our friends? Imagine a person who doesn't object to receiving a kindness from his friends, but it never enters into his head to do a kindness in return.

"Then there will be no value in him."

This brings to mind something that Antiphon once said to me:

"Socrates, I believe you are a good and upright man. But your so-called wisdom cannot have much value because you don't ask for payment for your time. And yet, if it were your cloak, or your house, or any other of your possessions, you would set some value on it and never dream of parting with it for free. If you thought your teaching was worth anything, then you would ask for it no less than its equivalent in gold. I conclude two things: First, you are a good man because you do not cheat people; second, you cannot be wise because your wisdom has no monetary value. Socrates, you are just a thinker; therefore, no use to anyone."

I asked Antiphon if it would be better if I were a thoughtless person. He had no reply, so the matter was dropped. But let's return to our discussion about friends, Critobulus. A sophist is someone who teaches a false-wisdom, the art of merely being able to win an argument at any cost. The sophist takes money, but the student learns nothing about truth or how to be a better person. Compare that with someone who recognizes the noble nature of another person, whose motive is to teach that other person the importance of reason, self-examination, discipline, honesty, and to strive always to achieve the best possible character. These are the actions of a true friend, and that should be the duty of every good citizen. In accordance with this idea, I take pleasure in good friends, and if I have any knowledge, I am happy to share it; but if I lack knowledge, then I recommend them to others by whom I think they will be helped on the path of virtue.

"So tell me, Socrates, what kind of person shall we endeavor to make our friend? What should we look for?"

Someone who has self-control, upright in all dealings, generous in kindness, and hopeful that his behavior is beneficial to his friends.

"But how are we to test these qualities in others, Socrates?"

How do you test the merits of a sculptor? Not by inferences drawn from the speech of the artist. No, we look to what he has already achieved. If the existing statues of his were nobly executed, we can trust he will do equally well with others.

"You mean that if we find someone whose kindness to his friends is established, we may take it as showing that he will treat his newer friends as amiably?"

Why not? If I see someone who has shown skill in the handling of horses, then I conclude that he will handle others no less skillfully. But of course these inferences do not guarantee with certainty that we will be right. This reasoning is different from adding sums or proving things about geometrical figures. Practical decisions and inferences have a built-in uncertainty. But since we must act on practical matters, we should do our best to seek out the relevant facts and evidence, so our inferences have the best chance of success. But even if we fail, we can still learn something.

> *"Let's suppose that we have discovered someone whose friendship is worth having. How are we to capture this person?"*

Capture? Not by running him down like a rabbit. Trying to capture someone against his will is wrong-headed. Those who are so treated are apt to become foes instead of friends.

> *"So, if we want to win the friendship of any good person, we need to be good ourselves in speech and action."*

And did you imagine that it was possible for a bad person to make good friends? You need only try to become good yourself, and when you have attained that, good friends will recognize you. This endeavor requires many steps. You must be devoted to your friends such that nothing gives you so much joy as a good friend; that you pride yourself no less for the fine deeds of those you love than on your own; and that you never weary of helping them.

"What is the best way to help your friends?"

There is but one road, the shortest and safest: In whatever you desire to be deemed good, endeavor to be good. Investigate all the virtues attainable by humans and you will find that all of them can be increased by learning and practice. All the noblest things which custom compels us to learn, and to which indeed we owe our knowledge of life, have all been learned by means of reason; and the best teachers are those who have the freest command of thought and language; and those who have the best knowledge of the most serious things are the most brilliant masters of conversation and examination. If we live up to the standard of our models, we may hope at least to match their excellence.

And another thing, if, as you claim, our friends can profit us, then perhaps all people do have a market value, since even the enemies of a person's household may be wealth to him, if he knows how to turn them to profit.

"That is my opinion."

In fact, you need but use your eyes to see how many private persons, not to say crowned heads, do owe the increase of their estates to war.

"Yes, but then they invariably become involved in endless difficulties."

114

I agree. Sooner or later they become enslaved by luxury, lechery, intemperance, and ruinous ambition. These passions so cruelly take control that the trapped person loses all freedom of thought. Eventually, he succumbs to new players on the stage, those even more devious than himself.

> *"I concede your point about placing a market value on our friends. But what about wealth in general? For example, given our different financial situations, do you claim that you have no need of further wealth?"*

My situation is amply sufficient to meet my needs, whereas you and the reputation you must live up to, would be barely well off, I take it, if what you have already were multiplied by three.

> *"How can that be?"*

First, you are called upon to offer many costly sacrifices, failing which, I take it, neither gods nor men would tolerate you. Second, you are bound to welcome numerous guests and to entertain them handsomely. Third, you must feast your fellow-citizens and ply them with all sorts of expensive delicacies, or else risk being cut adrift from them.

> *"I am willing to admit that I do live under those constraints, Socrates. You have given me much to think about, especially how I see people and physical objects, as though*

they were nothing but commodities to be bought and sold."

I, too, have learned much from our conversation. I thank you for spending your time with me. And I'm sure that Ischomachus, who joined us while we were talking, may be able to help us further the conversation because he knows about farming. Were you able to follow our discussion, Ischomachus?

"Yes, I did. If you don't mind, I have been pondering something that I would like to discuss. It concerns that which is beneficial to individuals and to society. Let me begin by saying that it seems to me that in every well-constituted city the citizens are not content merely to pass good laws, but they further choose the guardians of the laws, whose function as inspectors is to praise those whose acts are law-abiding and penalize those who acts are against the law. Therefore, those whose actions are beneficial to society are rewarded, but those whose actions are detrimental to society are punished."

If I follow you correctly, you claim that someone who strives by practice and training to be a just person may hope more fully to secure life's rewards. But now I need to understand some details. What particular toil do you impose on yourself in order to secure good health and strength? How do you take pains to create a surplus which will enable you to benefit your friends and to gratify the state?

> *"As far as I am able, I do good to many and hurt no one. For example, if some member of my household has some charge to bring, or some defense to make against another, I listen and examine the situation to determine the truth. On another occasion it may happen there is someone whom I have to blame or praise before my friends, or if I must arbitrate between some close friends, then I try to get them to agree that it is to their own interests to be friends, not foes."*

Suppose you must ask someone to take your place when you are absent from your home. Must that person have goodwill toward you and yours?

> *"A kindly disposition toward me and mine is precisely what I first endeavor to instill."*

This is exactly what I wish to learn from you. How do you teach that person to have kindly feelings toward yourself and yours?

> *"By treating that person kindly, Socrates."*

If I understand you, those who enjoy your kindness will grow well disposed to you and seek to render you some good.

> *"Yes, for of all the instruments to promote good feeling, this I see to be the best. Of course, I also teach them to be careful in the application of their duties."*

Now I am thoroughly intrigued. I always thought it was beyond the power of anyone to teach these virtues.

> *"I don't claim that it is possible to teach such virtues to every single person. I have no knowledge of that being the case."*

Do you have some idea what kind of people are capable of learning such virtues?

> *"I imagine you would have some difficulty in making intemperate people diligent. One kind of intemperance regards drunkenness which creates forgetfulness of everything that needs to be done."*

And are persons devoid of self-control the only ones incapable of diligence and carefulness? Or are there others?

> *"A person who is so lazy that he exists with eyes half-open is such that he cannot do right himself, or even comprehend when others do what is right."*

Are we to regard these as the only people incapable of being taught the virtue of carefulness? Or are there still others?

> *"Surely we must include the slave to love. A woeful lover is quite incapable of paying attention to anything beyond one single object. No light task, I take it, to discover any hope or occupation sweeter to him than that which now enthralls him; nor, when the call for action comes, will it be easy to invent worse punishment than that he now endures in separation from the object of his passion. Accordingly, I am in no great hurry to appoint a person of this sort to manage my affairs; the attempt to do so I regard as futile."*

And what of those addicted to another passion, that of gain? Are they, too, incapable of being trained to give attention to your affairs?

> *"On the contrary, these are the easiest people to train. You need only to point out to them that the pursuit is gainful, and their interest is aroused."*

But for ordinary people? Given they are sufficiently self-controlled to suit your bidding, and they have a wholesome appetite for gain, how will you teach them the virtue of carefulness?

"By a simple method, Socrates. When I see someone intent on carefulness, I praise and do my best to honor that person. On the other hand, when I see a person neglectful of his duties, I do not spare him; I try in every way, by word and deed, to punish him."

Please explain the teaching process itself. Is it possible for a person devoid of carefulness himself to teach others the virtue of carefulness?

"No more possible than for a person who knows no music to make others musical. If the teacher sets but an ill example, the pupil can hardly learn to do the thing correctly. And if the teacher's conduct is suggestive of laxity, how can his students learn to be careful?"

But now suppose you have convinced someone of being careful in the execution of your wishes. Is a person so qualified to be regarded as fit at once to represent your affairs? Or is there something else which he must learn in order to play the part of an efficient agent?

"It still remains for him to learn the particulars and methods of farming—to know what things he has to do, and when and how to do them. Ignorance of these details will assure failure."

But suppose he learns the whole routine of your business, will he need anything else, or have we found at last your perfect agent?

"He must learn how to rule the workers."

You mean to say that you educate your agents to that extent? You teach them to be capable of ruling others?

"I try to do so."

How do you manage to educate another in the skill of governing human beings?

"I have a simple system, Socrates; so simple, I daresay, you will simply laugh at me."

I assure you the matter is too important for me to laugh. Anyone who can make another capable of ruling others is capable of making that person grander still, a kingly being. This ability deserves the highest praise.

"Here are my thoughts on this matter, Socrates. Animals are taught obedience partly through punishment when they disobey and partly through some reward or kindness when they obey. This is the principle adopted in the breaking of young

horses. If the horse obeys its trainer, then something sweet is sure to follow, and if it disobeys, then some punishment follows. This pattern continues until the horse yields obedience to the trainer's every wish. The same method can be used for other animals such as dogs.

"But when it comes to humans, we have a being capable of persuasion through appeals to reason; for example, we can show him why it is in his best interest to obey. In fact, some people seek praise no less than others crave for fine food and drink. My practice then is to instruct those I desire to be my agents by the various methods which I have found to be successful in gaining the obedience of my fellows. For instance, since I provide clothes for my workers, I make sure that some clothing is better than others. My objective is that the clothes vary with the quality of the worker. The worse workers receive the worse clothes, and the better workers gets better clothes. After all, the better workers will become despondent seeing that their work is no more valued than the laziest workers. And I treat my agents the same way. If my agent succumbs to the flattery of a lazy worker, I do not let the matter pass; I reprimand him, thereby teaching him that such conduct is not in his best interest."

Well, then, suppose the man is now so fit to rule that he can compel obedience. Is he, I ask once more, your perfect agent, or is it that even though he has all the qualifications you have so far named, he still lacks something?

> "One thing is still required, and that is not to steal from me. The agent is the person through whose hands the harvests of my farm pass, so he must be honest and just in his actions."

You actually teach them the virtue of justice?

> "Of course. But it does not follow that I find everyone equally able to follow my instruction. What I do is this. I take a leaf now out of the laws of Draco and another out of the laws of Solon, and by so doing I start my household on a path of uprightness. And indeed, if I am not mistaken, those legislators enacted many of their laws expressly with a view to teaching this branch of justice. It is written, 'Let a person be punished for a deed of theft'; 'Let whosoever is detected in the act be bound and thrown in prison'; 'If he is violent, let him be put to death.' It is clear to me that the intention of the lawgivers in framing these enactments was to render the sordid love of gain devoid of profit to the unjust person. Therefore, I start with a sample of

these wise precepts, to which I supplement others taken from the royal code when they applicable; and so I do my best to shape the members of my household into the likeness of a just and honorable person concerning that which passes through their hands. I use different techniques for different people and situations because not everyone responds to the same kind of teaching. I give practical advice specific to situations.

"The laws act as penalties, as deterrents to transgressors, but the royal code aims higher, by it not only is the malefactor punished, but the righteous and just person is rewarded. The result is that a person can see how the just grow wealthier than the unjust, and even though he still might harbor in his heart some covetous desires, he can hold steadfast in his resolve to remain committed to virtue. To abstain from unjust dealings is thus engrained in him."

I understand. But now, suppose you have created in the character or soul of someone a desire for your welfare; have inspired in him not a mere passive interest, but a deep concern to help you to achieve prosperity. Further, you have taught him knowledge of the methods needed to give the operations of the estate a measure of success. You have, moreover, made him capable of ruling; and, as the crowning point of all your efforts, this same person shows no less delight than you might take yourself in laying at your feet earth's products, each in due season richly harvested. I need hardly ask concerning such a person whether anything else is lacking in him. It is clear to me an agent of this sort would be worth his weight in gold. But still, I ask that you not omit a topic somewhat lightly handled by us in the previous argument.

"What topic is that?"

It was said, unless I am mistaken, that it was important to learn the correct particulars and methods of farming because, you asserted, that unless a person knows what things he has to do and how to do them, all the virtues of carefulness and diligence and honesty will not, by themselves, lead to a successful outcome.

"What you are asking is how I teach the art of the correct preparation of land for growing crops?"

Yes, because now it looks as if this art made the possessor of it wealthy, but the unskilled, in spite of all the careful pains he takes, must live in poverty.

"I'll tell you the nature of this art. Since farming is of supreme utility to humans, it has a nobility in it; but, at the same time, it is the easiest of all the arts to learn."

I am easily persuaded that if I am to direct my care to farming, then I must have a knowledge of that art. But the bare recognition of the fact does not provide me with the knowledge how I ought to farm. And if I lacked that knowledge, then I would resemble a physician visiting my patients without knowing what to prescribe or what to do to ease their suffering. Therefore, to save me from such a predicament, please teach me the actual work and processes of farming.

> *"It is not with farming as with the other arts, where the student must be crushed beneath a load of study before turning out work of enough value to support his needs. On the contrary, the art of farming is not so hard to learn. Simply by watching laborers in the field, by listening to what they say, you will have enough clear knowledge to teach another. And further, I imagine, Socrates, that you yourself, although quite unconscious of the fact, already know a vast amount about the subject.*
>
> *"I also believe that, although there are some arts where the expert artist is disposed to keep his skills a secret, with farming it is different. Here the farmer who has the most skill in planting will take great pleasure in being watched by others; and so too the most skillful sower. Ask any question you may choose about farming and not one*

feature will the expert farmer seek to keep concealed."

An art so easy to be learned, you say? If so, can you explain its details to me. There is no shame on you who teach, but on me to lack knowledge of something as highly useful to the student as this.

"First then, Socrates, I wish to demonstrate to you that the so-called intricate variety in farming—a phrase used by those who lack practical experience of farming—actually presents no difficulty. What they assert is that anyone who would attempt farming must first be made acquainted with the true nature of soil."

And they are surely right in their assertion; for he who does not know what the soil is capable of bearing, can hardly know, I imagine, what he has to plant or what to sow.

"But Socrates, he has only to look at his neighbor's land, at his crops and trees, in order to learn what the soil can bear and what it cannot. After all, you cannot simply plant whatever you wish and hope that it grows, you can only grow what your particular soil can handle. Sometimes you have to look at a neighboring district to see what is commonly grown. Thus, even a person who has the barest

knowledge of the art of farming can still learn something of the nature of the soil."

Thank you. I am bold enough now to believe that no one need abstain from agriculture for fear he will not recognize the nature of the soil. Indeed, I now recall that those who fish in boats can judge the quality of the crops on lands that they pass, so they know whether the soil is good or bad. And this knowledge coincides with the verdict of the skilled farmer as to the quality of soil.

"At what point shall I begin then, Socrates, to show you how much about farming you already know? To explain to you the processes employed simply requires the acknowledgement of a hundred details which you already know full well."

The first thing I should like to learn, if only as a point befitting a philosopher, is this: How to proceed and how to work the soil if I desire to extract the largest crops of, for example, wheat and barley?

"Good. You are aware that to revive a soil that has been left unsown for a long time it must be plowed and harrowed in readiness for new sowing."

Yes, I am aware of that.

"Well then, suppose you wish to plow your land in winter."

That would not do; it would probably be too hard or too muddy.

"What about summer?"

The soil will be too hard in summer.

"So it looks as if springtime is the best season to begin this work?"

I expect that is the best season to plow the soil.

"When it comes to sowing, what is your opinion? Can you suggest a better time for sowing than that which the experience of former generations, combined with that of people now living, recognizes as the best? Do not sow on dry soil. Now I ask you: Is it better to plant everything at once?"

I imagine it should be spread out to avoid either too large a surplus or not enough to sustain one's needs.

"Then, on this point also, Socrates, we hold the same opinion—the pupil and the teacher; and what is more, the pupil was the first to give the answer."

I see your point.

>*"Should the seed be cast carefully by hand?"*

Of course.

>*"But as to actual scattering, is everyone equally adept?"*

No, the hand needs practice like the fingers of a harp player. After sowing, naturally we hope to come to reaping. If you have anything to say on that, please proceed to teach me.

>*"Yes, by all means, unless you prove on this also to know as much yourself already as your teacher. To begin then: You know that corn needs cutting?"*

To be sure, I know that much at any rate.

>*"In the act of cutting corn how will you choose to stand—facing the way the wind blows?"*

Not facing the wind because then my eyes and hands will suffer from being hit by the husks and particles of straw.

>*"There, Socrates, you know as much about it as I do myself."*

It appears so. But do I have sound knowledge about threshing?

"Well, I suppose you are aware of this much: The fact that corn is threshed by beasts of burden."

Yes, and "beast of burden" is a general term that includes oxen, horses, mules, and so forth.

"Is it your opinion that these animals know more than merely how to tread the corn when put to the task?"

What more need they know?

"Someone must see to it that the animals tread out what requires threshing and no more, and that the threshing is done evenly. Tell me, Socrates, who would you assign to that duty?"

Clearly it is the duty of the threshers who are in charge. It is theirs to finish off the work as fast as possible.

"Once again, your comprehension of the facts keeps pace with mine, so you are fully competent yourself, it seems, to teach as well."

Perhaps I must somehow know about these matters, though unconsciously. Our discussion, and your questions as a teacher on these matters, have somehow allowed me to piece together ideas that I was not aware that I had. But perhaps it is not a recollection of knowledge that I already had, but instead your questions triggered an ability to make connections between ideas that were held separate in my mind, or to impel me to create inferences from those ideas and thereby to discover new thoughts. Perhaps further that although the ability to make inferences may be inborn, it still requires specific experiences to advance knowledge of particular topics, such as farming. As far as teaching goes, no one ever taught me farming. But having lived long enough I sometimes observed farmers. Therefore, your teaching cultivated the soil and carefully brought the seeds of ideas to full bloom in my mind.

> *"Did I not tell you, Socrates, that farming was the noblest of all arts? It is also the most generous because it is the easiest to learn."*

Without a doubt. In the course of my life I must have gained an unconscious competence of agriculture. And now, through your teaching and patience, all these things I now consciously see. My experiences supplied me with memories of certain patterns, and my newfound agricultural knowledge was gained by being led through a series of questions whose purpose was to allow me to connect relevant scattered past occurrences into whole cloth.

But the practical needs of living in a changing physical world result only in temporary knowledge, that is, ideas, guesses, and predictions that change over time because our experiences change as the world changes. Our ideas about farming—such as when and what to plant—cannot guarantee success because the outcome is subject to drought, or too much rain, or blight, or insects, or fire, or other unforeseen conditions. We manage to succeed for a time, perhaps a long time, even through generations. We also know that things will eventually change, so we will have to adapt and adopt new ideas.

This is why I want to contrast practical knowledge with what I see as knowledge that is unchanging. For example, the way we understand justice, honesty, temperance, and other virtues. Are they learned through experience, trial and error, and through dialogue between willing and honest partners? Is this how societies have come about, by trying different kinds of laws and governance to see what works and what doesn't? And does this holds for individuals as well? Do we try different actions with different people, depending on our hopes, desires, and needs, in order to see what happens? And by this method, do we learn what works and what doesn't? Or are virtues so different from agriculture that they cannot be taught, and instead have to be recognized as true through reason alone? After all, what we know about agriculture is ever-changing; if the weather suddenly changes or the soil is eroded, our so-called knowledge is useless; it has to be replaced by a new understanding of how the physical world has changed.

> *"I understand, Socrates. Agriculture is an art that has to be adjusted depending on the changing circumstances of the world."*

Then can we really call it "knowledge?" I believe that knowledge should be of something permanent. Otherwise it is just a transitory fabric of guesses that are correct for a while, but then become incorrect. Skills regarding the physical world gained through experience are learned, but these are not permanent things. Given this, perhaps we should not call them "knowledge" because I want to reserve that term to refer to ideas that are unchanging eternal truths.

> *"I agree, Socrates."*

Can we also agree that virtues are of a nature completely different from temporary skills? Don't we understand and recognize wisdom, honesty, temperance, and truthfulness to be virtues because they have an eternal nature? And. as such, they are not learned through experience of an ever-changing world, but through reason which is the only way to glimpse their eternal nature?

> *"I see what you mean by the different natures of, for example, agriculture and honesty. It is clear agriculture is learned*

through experience, but, honesty seems to be something we understand only through thinking about ideas."

We learn and teach about physical processes, but since what we learn and teach is constantly changing, it is a mixture of skills and changing experience. It consists partly by the asking of questions, and, depending on the answers received, by pointing out analogies to what the student already understands or has experienced. Our ancestors learned farming through years of patient experimenting with soil, seeds, water, and sunlight to see what works. We are the inheritors of their experiences. But in contrast, honesty does not depend on changing circumstances. A true grasping of it requires a rational understanding of its eternal nature. ≈ ≈ ≈

≈ ≈ ≈ Meno, I didn't notice you had joined us. How long have you been here? Did you hear our conversation?

"I did, Socrates."

I imagine that I was so absorbed in conversation with Ischomachus that I didn't notice you. Do you wish to join the discussion?

"I would be delighted. Your conversation involved several topics about learning,

teaching, and knowledge that I am eager to discuss. For example, how I can inquire into that which I don't know, and if I find what I want, how will I ever know that this is the thing that I did not know?"

It seems that your question hides an argument, Meno. Someone cannot inquire either about that which he knows, or about that which he does not know, because if he knows, then he has no need to inquire; and if not, he cannot, for he does not know the subject about which he is to inquire.

"Well, Socrates, is the argument not sound?"

I don't think so.

"Why not?"

Questions about how we learn, how and what we can teach, and what counts as knowledge are intimately connected. There are arguments to the effect that at least some learning is based on past experience, for example the capacity to see connections between bits of memory that we gain through experience of the world. And there are other arguments to the effect that the ability to infer what may happen from what has happened, the capacity to derive logical consequences from accepted information, may already exist at birth. And still other arguments hold that what we learn about the physical world is not really knowledge; true knowledge is reserved for the eternal truths which are not, and cannot, be learned through experience; they can only be recognized through reason.

Let me spell out these positions, after which I will let you decide which of them you believe is correct. Let's examine what is implied by the third argument. If knowledge of eternal truths is possible—but if it can neither be taught nor learned—then perhaps we have it before we are born. This can happen if our souls are immortal. And having been born and reborn many times, and having seen all things that exist, the soul has an intimate knowledge of every eternal truth. Thus, experience, reflection, and what we call "teaching" is then simply recalling to mind what we already knew. In other words, the soul is able to "recover" all knowledge because what we call "teaching," "learning," and "inquiry" are simply the recollections of the eternal truths. An alternative way of saying the same point might be that our ability to reason is not learned, it is an essential part of us from birth. And it is that ability which allows the possibility of recognizing eternal truths.

Now let's contrast this with the idea that at least some knowledge is learned through experience. Although we are born with certain capacities—for example, the ability to recall past experiences, and the use of reason to create and analyze arguments—nevertheless, these abilities are activated only by our experiences which create the foundation of learning and teaching about the physical world. But since what we learn about the physical world is transitory, we should not call it knowledge.

> *"Please expand on this, Socrates, because I think I grasp some of what you are saying, but the subtleties probably escape me at this point. Can you help me get a better grasp of what you mean when you say that we do not learn, and that what we call learning is a process of recollection. Can you teach me how this is?"*

You are trying to trick me, Meno. If the position is correct, then I cannot teach you anything, at least as far as eternal truths are concerned.

> *"I assure you that I asked the question out of habit, not to trick you, Socrates. But if you can, show me how I can better understand the meaning of what you are saying."*

Let's try something. Suppose you call one of your attendants, so we can explore the question further by means of a practical demonstration.

> *"I'll call one of my servants."*

I will engage him in conversation by asking a series of questions. Let's observe whether he learns from me or merely remembers.

> *"A splendid idea, Socrates."*

Tell me, lad, do you know what a square figure looks like?

"Yes, I do."

And do you know that a square figure has four sides of equal length?

"Yes."

Now I want you to imagine the figures that I will talk about. Think about a square figure that has one vertical line and one horizontal line drawn through the middle of the square. Are those two lines equal?

"Yes, they are."

Of course, Meno, the lad had to have been taught the words I have been using. For example, the terms "square," "four," "equal," "vertical," "horizontal," and "lines" are words that he could not utter at birth. It is not the specific words that I want to concentrate on, but the underlying geometric principles at play. It is those that we are exploring to see if they, too, are learned or recollected.

"That is the issue at hand, Socrates."

Now tell me, lad, can a square be of any size?

"I think so."

Now imagine a square where one side of the square is two feet, and the other side is also two feet. Then that square would be twice two feet?

"Yes."

And how many are twice two feet?

"Four, Socrates."

Correct. And might there be another square twice as large as this one and having equal sides?

"Yes."

And how many feet will that be?

"Eight feet."

Correct again. Well done. What is the length of the line which forms the sides of a square of eight feet?

"It will be double the one with sides of two feet. So, the lines which form the sides of a square of eight feet will be four feet."

Observe, Meno, that I am simply asking him questions. At this point he thinks that he knows how long a line is needed to produce a figure of eight square feet, does he not?

"Yes."

But does he really know?

"No, his answer is incorrect."

He guesses that because the square is double, the line of a side is double.

"Yes, it is a guess based on what he understands up to this point."

Let's continue with the thought process. Tell me, lad, are you saying that a double space comes from a double line? Note that I am speaking of a square of eight feet, one that is twice the size of the original one of four feet. Do you still think that the double square comes from a double line?

"That still seems to make sense to me, Socrates."

Let's think about what you are saying. Does the line of a side become doubled if we add another such line?

"Yes, it does."

And four such lines will make a space containing eight feet?

"I believe it will."

I want you to imagine such a figure. Try to capture it in your mind. There are now four divisions in this new figure, each of which is equal to the figure of four feet. Do you agree?

"Yes."

And is not that four times four?

"It is."

And is that what we wanted?

"No, there are now sixteen, not eight."

So we have created a figure that is *four times* our original, not one that is double.

"I see that now."

Therefore, doubling the line has created a space, not twice, but four times as much.

"Yes, it did."

At this point we know that a space of four feet is made from the side of our original square. Now we know that doubling the original side creates a space of sixteen feet. So, can we say that a space of eight feet is twice the original square but half the new square?

"That must be right."

Such a space, then, will be made out of a side greater than the first one but less than the second one.

"Yes."

Then the line that forms the side of eight feet must be more than the line of two feet, but less than the one of four feet.

"It must be."

See if you can tell me how much it will be.

"Three feet."

I want you to go back to our original square of four feet. Hold that in your mind. Now add half of the side of two feet to each side of the square. How long is each side now?

"Three feet."

Picture that in you mind.

"I have it."

This new square has three feet in one direction and three feet in the other direction. How many feet will be in this square?

"Nine. I can see that clearly in my mind."

We know, now, that the figure of eight feet, which is what we want, is not made out of a side of three. Based on what we have done, can you now see the correct answer?

"No, Socrates, I have no idea."

Do not despair, you have made a lot of progress. See, Meno, what advances he has made. He did not know at first, and he does not know now, what is the side of a figure of eight feet. But he thought that he knew, and he answered confidently as if he knew. Now he is stuck, and he neither knows nor thinks that he knows. But isn't he better off in knowing that he doesn't know? If the questioning has made him doubt, then have we done him any harm?

> *"No. He is at a point where he won't delude himself into thinking that he knows something when he does not. In fact, I would say that is a healthy attitude for anyone to have."*

It seems that we assisted him in some degree to the discovery of the truth. And now he will wish to remove his doubt. But again, let's observe carefully whether we are teaching him something that he didn't know, or whether we are merely helping him recollect that which he already knew.

Now, lad, let's start over again with our original square of four feet. Do you have it in your mind?

"Yes, I do."

Do you recall the image that you created by doubling each side of that square?

"Yes. It was a square of sixteen feet."

Correct. Now make sure you understand that the square of sixteen feet is made up of four of the original four-foot squares.

"I understand that."

Now focus just on the bottom left square of four feet. In your mind draw a straight line from the upper left corner of that square to the bottom right corner of that square.

"I have it."

Do you see agree that this new line has cut that one square of four feet in half?

"Yes, it cut that square in half. I can see that."

Now go back to the upper left corner of that square to the point where you started drawing the new line.

"I have it."

From that point draw a straight line to the upper right corner of the square above it.

"Done."

What has this new line done to the upper left square of four feet?

"It has cut it in half."

Correct. Now draw a line from the upper right corner of the square you just finished with to the bottom right of the square of four feet that is next to it.

"I have done it."

What has this new line done to the upper right square of four feet?

"It has cut it in half, too."

We are almost done. You need only to draw one more line. Draw a line from the bottom right corner of the square you just finished with to the bottom left corner of the square below it.

"I have done it. And I see that it has cut that square in half, too."

I'm happy to hear that you have anticipated and correctly answered what would have been my next question.

Look carefully at the four new lines you have drawn in your mind. You already understand that these four new lines have cut each of four squares of four feet in half.

"Yes, I can see that clearly."

And are these four new lines of equal length?

"Yes, they are."

I want you focus just on those four equal lines. Do they create a new space?

"Yes, they do. And that new space is also a square."

Wonderful. And each of the four new lines cut in half the space in each of the four squares of four feet.

"Yes, they cut each in half."

Then how big is the new space created by the four new lines?

"I don't know."

You agreed that the four new lines cut each of the four spaces in half. And how many spaces were there in the large area?

"Sixteen."

If the four new lines cut each space in half, then how big is the new area?

"Eight feet! Now I understand."

And is this what we wanted?

"Yes, it is."

I can now teach you a new word; the new lines are called "the diagonal." As we have shown, the double space that we were looking for resulted from a square made of the four diagonals.

What do you think, Meno? Did I teach him, or did he simply remember?

> *"I'm not sure. As you said earlier, someone had to teach him the basic words that you used to refer to the lines and spaces. Your questions seemed to be a combination of taking what he knew and extending it to places he clearly did not know. But then he was able to understand the process and he seemed at times to be recollecting some distant knowledge, or perhaps deducing things which he did not previously know,*

148

I'm not sure which. If the latter, then in some sense you did teach him something that he did not know. I think we can agree that he could not recollect just anything. I mean he couldn't know what you ate for dinner last week. How could he know things like that?"

You have captured the problem perfectly, my friend. Specific things about the world can be learned through experience. But these are fleeting things, they have no permanence as knowledge. I believe we are capable of going beyond the physical world, beyond the constant flux of temporary experience that changes constantly, and through reason and honest striving, snatch a glimpse of permanent truths, such as the geometric examples we looked at.

Although I had to rely on his imagination, the ideas that were brought out regarding areas, squares, and lines go beyond any actual drawings to reveal an ideal world of geometry that can be understood in the mind. Our drawings of geometrical figures are crude shadows of the ideal squares and lines that can be understood only through reason. We are like archers who try to hit the center of a target but often miss. Like archers, those aiming to live a virtuous life need to know what the center of the target is; but those centers are not physical objects that our eyes can see, they are ideal centers that can be recognized only by our minds.

As we saw when the lad finally saw the answer to the square problem, some knowledge is unchanging, including geometry and mathematics, where once we recognize the truth we know that it is immutable. This recognition contrasts with our beliefs regarding the nature of the physical world that we follow until they fail.

The difference is stark. The eternal truths cannot be experienced through our senses, they can be recognized only in the mind. And once we recognize such a truth, our minds touch eternity. But since our bodies drag us back to the world of senses because of our bodily needs, the mind-glimpses of eternal truths are evanescent. Nevertheless, the effort is worth it, if we want to know what is true.

Since the truths I am talking about are eternal and unchanging, they cannot be part of the physical world that is always changing. We can recognize the eternal truths through our minds, but the recognition and understanding of their eternal nature is completely different from the kinds of things we learn about the physical world. The recognition is immediate, absolute, and is ascertained instantly as if we knew it all along.

The reason that anyone can recognize geometrical and mathematical truths is that they are not invented by us, they exist independently. But the same cannot be said of how we deal with the physical world. Each of us learns specific aspects of the physical world through our individual experience, which, of course, we can transmit to others. This is how agriculture is handed down from generation to generation. But since each generation has to deal with the physical world's inevitable changes, information regarding successful agriculture changes. Not so with geometry and mathematics. Those truths are permanent, so each generation recognizes the same truths.

As we worked through the problem, the lad suddenly saw the answer, an answer that seemed buried somewhere inside him. My questioning merely brought it to the surface, as if he always had this knowledge. So, did I teach him, or did he simply recollect? Knowledge lies in an eternal realm of being that we can access through rational thought. But it is a difficult process. ≈ ≈ ≈

≈ ≈ ≈ Oh, I see that Glaucon has joined our group. Did you hear our conversation about the squares, Glaucon?

"I did, Socrates. Are you willing to take the discussion in a different direction, to the question of why we should be good? Along the way we might see whether the ideas we discuss are teachable. So, are you willing to take up the challenge to defend the idea that we should be good because it is the right thing to do? And are you willing to argue in support of the idea that being a moral or just person has intrinsic value, that it has value in itself regardless of the outcome of our actions?"

If I understand the challenge, I must try to persuade you that being just is always better than being unjust.

"Yes, but first we should try to clarify the nature of justice and injustice. Setting aside for the moment the rewards and consequences connected to just and unjust acts, I want to know what they are in themselves, and how they affect us. So in order to begin, let me relate arguments I heard about the nature and origin of justice. These arguments claim that everyone who practices justice does so against his will. I will then present further arguments to show that the life of an unjust person is often far better than the life of a just person.

"Although I am not convinced of these arguments, nevertheless I have not yet heard better arguments to the effect that justice is superior to injustice. I want to hear justice praised in respect of itself, then I shall be satisfied. And I believe you are the person most likely to do this. So, Socrates, I will do my best to argue that the unjust life is the best, and you are to argue the opposite. Do you agree to my proposal?"

Indeed I do, for I cannot imagine any more important topic for discussion.

"Then let me begin by discussing the nature and origin of justice. Some have claimed

that to do an injustice is good, but to suffer an injustice is bad. Moreover, the bad is far greater than the good. Further, when people have experienced bad and good effects, and when they realize they cannot always avoid the bad and obtain the good, then they think that they had better agree among themselves to have neither. This thinking leads to laws and mutual agreements; that which is ordained by law is lawful and just. This is affirmed by many to be the true origin and nature of justice. It is a compromise between the best of all, which is to do injustice and not be punished, and the worst of all, which is to suffer injustice without the power of retaliation. And since justice is a middle point between the two, it is tolerated not as a good, but as the lesser evil. Therefore, it is the consequence of the inability of certain people to bring themselves to do injustice. Such is the account held by many of the nature and origin of justice. Given this, those who practice justice do so involuntarily. In other words, people are diverted onto the path of justice by the force of law.

"And now I will relate a famous story to support that view. There was once a shepherd, Gyges by name, who was in the service of the king of Lydia. One day a small earthquake made an opening in the earth

near where Gyges was grazing his flock. He decided to explore the opening. After going down quite far, he came upon the dead body of a man with a gold ring on one finger. Gyges removed the ring and returned to the surface.

"Later that night, Gyges met with a group of other shepherds. While others were engaged in talk, Gyges happened to spin the ring on his finger so the gemstone was no longer showing. As soon as he did this, Gyges became invisible. The others simply thought that Gyges had wandered off somewhere. When he spun the ring again so the gemstone was showing, Gyges reappeared. He began thinking about the strange power that he now possessed. He realized that he could do almost anything he wanted while invisible and never be caught.

"Gyges volunteered to be one of the messengers who were sent to the king's court. Soon he contrived to test his power. Becoming invisible, he eventually managed to seduce the queen and kill the king. The queen eventually conspired with Gyges, probably out of fear, to take over the kingdom.

"Now suppose there were two such magic rings. And suppose that a just person put on one of them, and an unjust person put on the other. Can anyone imagine that he is of such an iron nature that he would never succumb to unjust acts? Wouldn't the realization that you would never be caught be too strong a temptation? If so, then the future actions of a just person who had the ring would be the same as the actions of an unjust person; they would come at last to the same point.

"Perhaps this story shows that someone is not willingly a just person, not because he thinks that justice is any good to him, but only out of necessity, for whenever anyone thinks that he can safely be unjust, he will be unjust. If so, then perhaps it is true that everyone believes in their hearts that injustice is far more profitable than justice, and he who argues as I have been supposing will say that they are right. If you could imagine anyone obtaining the power of becoming invisible but never doing any wrong, he would be thought by others to be an idiot.

"Now, if we are to form a real judgment of the life of the just and unjust, we must look at them separately. Let the unjust man be entirely unjust, and the just man entirely just, and they are to be perfectly rewarded for the work of their lives. Like Gyges, it is possible for an unjust man to act in such a way that the true nature of his acts lie hidden. In this extreme case, the unjust person might be thought by others to be just because any misdeeds would be covered up

155

*by his successful accumulation of money
and his ability to buy those eager to do his
bidding.*

*"In contrast, let us look at the just man in
his nobleness and simplicity, wishing, as
Aeschylus says, to be good and not simply
to appear good. Therefore, let him be
clothed in justice. And he can be imagined
in a state of life opposite of the former. Let
him be the best of men, but let him be
thought of as the worst; then he will have
been put to the test and we shall see whether
he will be affected by the fear of infamy and
its consequences. And let him continue
being a just person to the hour of death, but
appearing by others to be unjust. When both
men have reached this point, the one just
and the other unjust, let judgment be given
which of them is the happier of the two."*

Well done, Glaucon! How energetically you polish
the arguments as if they were two great gems.

*"I try my best, Socrates. And now that we
know what these two men are like, on what
principle, then, shall we any longer choose
justice rather than injustice? Knowing all
this, Socrates, how can anyone be willing to
honor justice, or indeed to refrain from
laughing when he hears justice praised?
And even if there should be someone who is
able to disprove the truth of my words, and*

who is satisfied that justice is best, still he is not angry with the unjust, but is ready to forgive them.

"Socrates, I know that you firmly believe that justice is good in itself, so I ask you to regard one point, namely, the essential good and evil that justice and injustice do to those who have them. Prove to us that justice is better than injustice, and show what those two things do to the individuals that makes one good and the other evil, regardless of whether this can be seen or unseen by gods and men."

Glaucon, your eloquence has created a vivid picture of the power and quality of justice and injustice. Now let's use our imagination to create an image of a person's character, or soul, whichever term is more pleasing to you.

"What kind of image do you mean?"

An image like the composite creations of ancient mythology, such as the Cerberus or Chimera in which two or more different natures are said to grow into one.

"I understand your meaning now."

Imagine a many-headed monster, having a ring of heads of all manner of beasts, tame and wild, which he is able to generate and metamorphose at will.

"You assume marvelous powers in the artist, Socrates, but since language is more pliable than wax, let there be such a model as you propose."

Excellent. Suppose now that you make a second form of a lion, and a third form of a man, the second smaller than the first monster, and the third smaller than the second.

"That is an easy task to imagine."

And now join them, and let the three images grow into one.

"Done."

Next, fashion the outside of them into a single image of a human. Thus, since no one can see inside the image, everyone believes it to be a single human.

"I have done what you ask."

And now, to those who maintain that it is profitable for the human to be unjust, and unprofitable to be just, let us reply that, if this is right, then it is profitable for this creature to feed the multitudinous monster and to strengthen the lion, but to starve and weaken the man who is consequently liable to be dragged about at the mercy of either of the other two. And he is not to attempt to familiarize or harmonize

158

them with one another—he ought rather to get them to fight each other to see who is strongest.

> *"Those who approve of injustice will say that."*

In contrast, the supporter of justice says that he should always speak and act so the man within the image has the most complete mastery over the entire creature. He should keep close watch over the many-headed monster, fostering and cultivating the gentle qualities, while also preventing the wild ones from growing; he should make the lion his ally, and in common care of them he should be uniting the several parts with one another and with himself.

> *"I imagine that someone who approves of justice would say this."*

Then from every point of view, whether of pleasure, honor, or advantage, the approver of justice is right and speaks the truth, and the disapprover is wrong and false and ignorant.

> *"I'm not sure this is enough to sway the supporters of injustice, Socrates."*

Then let us gently reason with the unjust person, who is not intentionally in error. We will say to him, "What is your conception of things noble and ignoble? Isn't the noble that which subjects the wild beast to the man, and the ignoble that which subjects the man to the wild beast?" How might he answer?

"He might agree in principle, Socrates, but still maintain that life is so hard that we sometimes have to dispense with principle."

If he agrees in principle, then we can ask him the following questions: How would a person profit if he received gold on the condition that he was to enslave the noblest part of him to the worst? Can anyone imagine that a person who sold his son or daughter into slavery for money, especially if he sold them into the hands of fierce and evil men, would be the gainer, no matter how large the sum which he received? And will anyone say that he is not a miserable and despicable person who remorselessly sells his own being to that which is detestable?

"That kind of profit would be difficult to defend, Socrates."

And we can say this to him: Isn't it true that when pride and anger grows and gains strength, when the wild beast within the image grows ever more rapacious, that many suffer? And isn't someone who uses false flattery, or who fans the flames of hatred and dissention among society out of sheer cruelty, mean-spiritedness, or narcissism, simply for the sake of money and power of which he can never have enough, isn't that person doomed to a solitary life in fear that others will eventually overtake him?

"All true enough. But the difficult task is to get that person to see the fate that awaits him."

Yes, but we must never stop trying. We must hold fast to the idea that being ruled by the best part of us, namely our reason, is the only possible way to wisdom and truth, neither of which we have to fear, no matter what our age. This way of living eliminates the fear of encountering the unknown. Gaining wisdom far outweighs monetary gain.

"I agree, Socrates. I just wish more people did."

This is clearly the intention of the law, which is the ally of the entire city. And it is also seen in the authority which we exercise over children, and the refusal to let them be free until we have established in them a principle analogous to the constitution of a state, whereby the rights and duties of all are to be respected and nurtured, and when this is done they may go their own way.

"Yes, the purpose of the law is clear."

From what point of view, then, and on what ground can we say that a man is profited by injustice or intemperance or other baseness, which will make him a worse man, even though he acquires money or power by his wickedness?

"From no point of view at all."

What shall he profit if his injustice goes undetected and unpunished? Those who go undetected get worse, whereas those who are detected and punished have a chance to change the brutal part of their nature, to release the gentler element in themselves, to become noble by acquiring justice and temperance and wisdom which last far longer than temporary pleasure, greed, or power.

People are capable of devoting the energies of their lives in order to attain the noble purpose of wisdom. They will honor the kind of learning which impresses these qualities on their characters. They will look at the city that is within themselves, and make sure that no disorder occurs in it.

By succumbing to the power of the ring of invisibility, Gyges became a tyrant, a person who seizes power by force and exercises it as he pleases. But an unjust person who is a slave to his unquenchable desires can never truly be happy or fulfilled no mater how long he lives. As the story of the ring shows, anyone who attains immense power will by any means necessary strive to keep it through corruption, bribery, and murder, or by rewriting the laws to protect himself and punish anyone who challenges him.

Although the Gyges story is enclosed in myth, the force behind it is to make us realize that many real people do in fact act like Gyges. But as I tried to show, chasing desires is a fool's task because the chase never ends. We can never be truly satisfied because we are miserable as long as a desire remains unfulfilled. And we are miserable after we attain the object of our desire because we soon become bored. This cycle has no end. This is why self-control, temperance, and wisdom are the intrinsic virtues that lead us to being good; they draw on what makes us unique—our ability to reason. To use reason not for outward physical gain, but to go beyond what our senses tell us about the world, to understand that which we cannot see—the eternal truths. The ring of Gyges will enslave us in a never-ending and unattainable quest for physical pleasure. Wisdom can lead to money, power, and physical pleasure, but money, power, and physical pleasure cannot lead to wisdom.

We must first improve ourselves before we can think about improving society. I know that it is difficult to reconcile practical knowledge with more elusive kinds such as justice, honesty, reverence, and the like. We have general agreement on the proper work or function of many kinds of practical knowledge. For example, carpentry, medicine, and farming require essential skills that are measured objectively by successful results. Is it possible, then, to describe the proper work or function of justice and honesty in a similar way? Can we talk about people who are just and honest the way we talk about doctors and shipbuilders, that is, by looking at the outcome of their actions? And since doctors and shipbuilders are expected to strive to be better professionals, so their actions result in better products, shouldn't we expect everyday people to strive to ensure that their actions are just and honest? If so, the results of everyone's actions should result in a better society because that is the proper function of justice and honesty. And isn't this a practical determination?

A just person works for himself in that his character is improved by being virtuous; in fact, being virtuous makes sense through our actions. Being virtuous by not interacting with others makes little sense. A person is considered just and honest depending on his actions, his behavior toward others. This means that being good or virtuous requires actions toward others. Being frugal, temperate, and taking care of your body has the effect of making you less likely to commit unjust acts—you won't be greedy, or rapacious, or slothful—thus making sure you are not an undue burden on society. ≈ ≈ ≈

≈ ≈ ≈ Crito, my good friend, why didn't you wake me as soon as you arrived?

> *"I did not wake you, Socrates, because I didn't want to disrupt your peaceful sleep. I have always thought of you as a happy person, but I am amazed to see how peaceful you seem in the face of this tragedy."*

Crito, when someone has reached my age, he

shouldn't worry about the approach of death.

"But others who found themselves in similar situations were distraught."

That may be true. But tell me, why did you come at this early hour?

"We are running out of time, Socrates."

You mean the ship has come from Delos, on whose arrival I am to die?

"No, the ship has not yet arrived, but it will probably be here today. If so, then tomorrow, Socrates, will be the last day of your life. Therefore, I beg you once more to take my advice and escape. If you die, I will not only lose a friend who can never be replaced, but many people who do not know us will believe that I might have saved you if I had been willing to give money for your escape. Now, can there be a worse disgrace than this—that I should be thought to value money more than the life of a friend?"

Why should we care about their opinion? Good people, and they are the only ones worth considering, will not think that way.

"But Socrates, we must consider the opinion of the majority of people because

> *what has happened to you shows that they can do the greatest evil to anyone they are against."*

If they can do the greatest evil, then they can also do the greatest good—and what a fine thing that would be. But in reality they can do neither—they cannot make someone wise, the greatest good, or foolish, the greatest evil.

> *"I will not argue with you, Socrates. But please tell me whether you are not acting out of regard to me and your other friends. Are you afraid that if you escape from prison, then we may get into trouble for helping you, that we will lose our property or be punished in some other way? If that is the case, then put it out of your mind because in order to save you we will definitely take that risk."*

That is one consideration, but by no means the only one.

> *"My resources are at your service, and many others will help, too. Therefore, do not hesitate on our account, and don't say, as you did in court, that it will be hard for you to live elsewhere. There are many people abroad who will take care of you and protect you. I cannot believe that you are justified in betraying your own life when*

you might be saved. In acting that way you are playing into the hands of your enemies. You are also deserting your own children. Instead of raising and educating them, you will die and leave them without a father. No one should bring children into the world who is unwilling to persevere in their nurture and education to the end. Of course, the trial should never have happened. But this last act will seem to have occurred through our negligence and cowardice. You can save yourself. With our help it will not be difficult. The time for deliberation is over. There is only one thing to be done, and it must be done tonight."

My dear Crito, your enthusiasm is invaluable—if what you say is right. But if you are wrong, then the greater the enthusiasm the greater the danger. The possibility of escape is not something to be taken lightly. Therefore, we should discuss the issue calmly because you know that I must be guided by reason, and now that this chance has come up, I cannot turn my back on reason. So, let's think what will be the fairest way to consider the question. Perhaps we should return to your argument about the opinion of the people. The question I want to consider is this: Should my beliefs and principles change because I am about to die? That is what I want to discuss with your help. Since you are not going to die tomorrow, you can be neutral and objective regarding the reasoning concerned. The argument is that the opinion of people should sometimes be followed, but at other times rejected. Is that right?

"Yes."

The good opinions should be followed, but not the bad.

"Yes."

And the opinions of wise people are good and should be given serious consideration, but the opinions of unwise people are bad and should not be seriously considered.

"Of course."

Let's explore some examples. Should a student learning to play the flute listen to the opinion of everyone, or just the flute teacher?

"The teacher."

And should the student take seriously the criticism, and welcome the praise of the teacher, or of everyone?

"Just the teacher."

And if the student disobeys and disregards the teacher and instead listens to those who have no knowledge of how to play the flute, then what will happen?

"The student will suffer."

Let's look at another example. Suppose you are sick. Should you go to a doctor, or ask your neighbors for advice?

"The doctor is the expert whose advice I would seek."

Then doesn't the same principle hold for others things as well, Crito? In questions of what is just and unjust, and good and evil, should we follow the opinion of those who have no expertise or knowledge, or should we follow the opinion of the person who has understanding?

"The one who has understanding."

And will life be worth having if we follow the wrong advice?

"No."

Then, my friend, we must not regard what most people may say. We must look at what someone who has understanding of justice and injustice says, and what truth tells us.

"But Socrates, you know all too well that the opinion of the majority can lead to the

death of anyone who is deemed a threat to them."

That is quite true. But which is better—to merely live, or to live a good life?

"To live a good life."

And is a good life equivalent to a just and honorable one?

"Yes, of course."

Let's see where our reasoning takes us, Crito. If we can determine that I am justified in escaping, then I will do it; but if not, then I will stay here. Several things that you mentioned—money, loss of character, the duty of educating one's children— these are the things that the majority of people would consider if they were in my place, wouldn't they?

"Yes."

But we who reason, and who do not act merely on emotions, must consider only whether my escape is justified or not. Nothing else is important. But in order to do that, we must first answer this important question: Is intentionally doing wrong always evil and dishonorable?

"Yes, it is."

170

So, we should not injure someone just because we have been injured. In fact, we should never injure anyone.

"I agree."

And what of doing evil in return for evil—which many people believe—is that justified?

"No, although I sometimes find myself captured by an emotional response to an evil that has been committed."

That is quite a natural response, Crito. But since we are capable of going beyond those initial emotional feelings, can we agree that doing evil to others is the same as injuring them?

"It is."

Then we should not retaliate or render evil for evil to anyone, whatever evil we may have suffered.

"I agree, we should not retaliate."

Good. Then we need now to answer this question: Should we do what we believe to be right, or should we betray it?

"We should do what we believe is right."

If that is true, then we can apply it to my situation. If

I escape prison against the will of the Athenians, have I wronged them? Or do I instead wrong those I ought least to wrong? In other words, do I desert the principles which were acknowledged by us to be just?

> *"I'm afraid that I don't know the answer, Socrates."*

Perhaps we should look at it in a different way. Let's consider an imaginary situation where the Spirit of the Laws visits our thoughts. Suppose that as I am considering avoiding some legal punishment, the Spirit of the Laws comes to me and says, *"Socrates, your action aims to overturn the laws and the state. Do you think the decisions of law have no power, and can be easily set aside and trampled upon by individuals?"* What will be my answer to this question, Crito? Should I reply that the state has injured me and given me an unjust sentence?

> *"Yes, you should say that."*

But then the Laws will say to me, *"And was that our agreement with you, Socrates? Were you expected to abide by the sentence of the state?"* If I declined to answer, then the Laws will add, *"Socrates, you spent your life asking and answering questions, so why do you hesitate at this moment? Tell us what complaint you have against us that justifies you in attempting to harm us and the state. Isn't it true, Socrates, that your parents' marriage was officiated by us? Do you have any objection to our regulating marriage?"* What could I say, Crito, except that I have no objection. Then the Laws will continue: *"Socrates, do you object to our regulating the nurturing and education of children, in which you were trained? Weren't the laws, which have charge of education, right in commanding your parents to educate you?"* I would have to say in all honesty that the Laws were right to do this. Of course, then the Laws will say, *"Well then, Socrates, since you were brought into the world and nurtured and educated by us, can you deny that you are also our child, just as your ancestors were before you? If this is true, then you do not have the right to harm anyone because you were harmed by them—only the state and the laws have that right and duty. At your trial, you were found guilty and condemned to die. Because of that outcome, do you now believe that you are justified in harming us in return? Will you, the philosopher of virtue, pretend that you are justified in this? Has a philosopher such as you failed to discover that the state and the laws should be revered by all those who claim to have wisdom? Otherwise, you must change your view of what is just. And if you may not do violence to your parents, then you may not do violence to your country."* Now tell me, Crito, how should I answer? Do the Laws speak truly, or do they not?

"It seems that they do."

Then the Laws will continue: *"Consider then, Socrates, whether you are going to injure us. Having*

173

brought you into the world, nurtured and educated you, given you and every other citizen a share in every good which we had to give, we further proclaim to every Athenian the liberty by which they are permitted to leave if they wish. But, if you choose to stay, then you willingly enter into a contract to do as the laws command. You, Socrates, of all Athenians, should know this." Upon hearing this I might ask the Laws why I, among all Athenians, should know this. They will answer, *"Because, Socrates, you accepted the contract long ago. There is clear and ample proof of this fact. You have lived here for over seventy years. You had your children and raised them here. During your trial you could have proposed exile as your penalty. More than likely, this would have been granted. But, instead, you pretended that you preferred death to exile, and that you were willing to die. Have you quickly forgotten your actions and words? Have you no respect for the Laws, whom you now wish to harm? Now you want to run away and turn your back upon the agreements which you freely made as a citizen—we did not force you. If you disagreed with any of the laws, then you had the right, and indeed the obligation, to make them better. Since you spent your time talking to others, you could have devoted some of your time to discussing which laws you found objectionable, and perhaps offered ways to rescind those laws, or have them rewritten to ensure fairness for all citizens. Now please answer this question, Socrates: Are we right in saying that you agreed to be governed according to us in deed, and not in word only? Is that true or not?"* How then shall I answer, Crito? Must I not agree?

> *"You cannot help it, Socrates. You must agree."*

Of course, my friend. Then the Laws will say, *"Consider the consequences of your actions, Socrates. Your friends may also be driven into exile; they may be stripped of their citizenship; they may lose their property, or be sent to prison. You will enter another country labeled as an enemy of laws. And if you are a corrupter of the laws, then perhaps it is true that you are a corrupter of the youth. Is your existence worth having on these terms? Aren't you ashamed to violate the most sacred laws simply because you desire to live a little longer? You will live—but what kind of life will it be? Listen, Socrates, to we who have raised you. Don't think of life first and of justice afterwards, but of justice first, that your actions may be justified. If you depart in innocence—as a sufferer and not a doer of wrong— then you will be a victim, not of the laws, but of misguided and unwise men."* What then, Crito?

> *"I'm sorry, Socrates, I don't know what to say."*

Thank you, my friend, for helping me think through these important questions. And please be sure to let my other friends know how we reasoned through the offer to help me escape. They may disagree, but I know that you will do your best to help them continue the conversation. ≈ ≈ ≈

≈ ≈ ≈ Now that the leg iron has been removed, I notice how curious it is that pain is so closely related to pleasure. They seem to be opposites because we don't experience them at the same time, and yet, when we encounter one, the other follows. I know by my present experience where the pain in my leg, caused by the heavy leg iron, is now subsiding, and the rubbing of the skin is becoming pleasurable.

It is strange how random thoughts occur when we are near death. Those who pursue philosophy should be unafraid of death. To my friends I say please do not give up too easily, for understanding may come at any time. And since I am soon going to another place, it is fitting that I reflect on the nature of the journey that I am about to take. I cannot think of anything better I would like to do from now until sunset, at which time I will be obliged to take my leave.

Many people accept that there are times when a certain event is considered evil, and other times it is considered good, with the exception of death. But aren't there times when it is better for some people to die? And, if so, why can't they take their own lives, instead of waiting for someone else to do it, or to let nature take its course?

"Socrates, do you mean that if someone is

in constant horrible pain, then maybe it would be all right to commit suicide instead of waiting for a natural, but painful, death? You now seem to be advocating something different from what you told us in the past. You often said that those with the philosophic spirit should go quickly and quietly to their death, but yet you also said that they shouldn't commit suicide. Isn't this a contradiction?"

I admit the appearance of inconsistency in what I said, but perhaps there is no real inconsistency. I once heard this idea: "*Humans are like prisoners who have no right to escape.*" I must admit that this poses a puzzle that I may not quite grasp. Nevertheless, in support of the idea, perhaps the gods are our guards, and that we are their prized possessions. If so, we can turn the question on its head. Suppose one of your own possessions—your dog or cat, for example—somehow decided to take the liberty of killing itself, even though you had no desire for it to happen. Would you be angry or confused? Would you do your best to stop the act? Whether we should wait for death to occur naturally, or whether it is acceptable for humans to take their own lives, reveals that philosophical questions are best decided after long contemplation.

I am quite ready to admit that I ought to be saddened at the prospect of my death; that is a normal, emotional reaction. But either I am going to a place where wise and good people go, perhaps some far better place for those who led good lives than for those who were evil, or else I will become nothing, and it will be like an endless and perfectly sound sleep. Either way, I intend to be true to philosophy to the bitter end—a perhaps ironic phrase since I am told that hemlock does have a rank odor and probably does taste bitter. But I am not bitter about my fate.

Philosophy and philosophers are quite often misunderstood. Many people fear the topics that philosophers are so eager to discuss. They view philosophers as morbid, depressing, pessimistic thinkers who relish talking about death, suffering, pain, whether gods exist, whether we can agree on moral acts, and on and on. Those people think that the tentative conclusions and seemingly eternal doubts of philosophers accurately reveal the truth about philosophers, and why they are feared, hated, and persecuted.

Please, will someone among you tell me your thoughts regarding death? Do you believe that it is the separation of soul and body, or consciousness and body, the separation of the physical from the non-physical parts of you?

"Yes, death is the separation of the physical from the non-physical."

Fine, so let's assume that we have a physical and non-physical existence. If so, then death results in the complete and final separation of the two parts, when they are released from each other and exist on their own.

"That is where the argument should begin."

Now, what shall we say about the attainment of knowledge? While we are alive, is the body a hindrance or a help in attaining knowledge? For example, do the senses of vision and hearing give us a perfectly accurate picture of the world? Or are they like the poets are always telling us, "inaccurate witnesses of reality"? And if they are not capable of discerning true reality, then what is to be said of the other senses? Isn't it true that thought and reason work best when the mind is able to shield itself from the constant intrusions of the body, so neither sounds, nor sights, nor pain, nor any pleasure trouble it; when it takes temporary leave of the body, and has as little as possible to do with it?

"As for myself, Socrates, I believe that my thoughts are clearest when I am able to attain some quiet, so my thoughts can focus undisturbed."

Let's expand your claim. It appears that the body not only constrains us individually, it also has social consequences. Wars are caused by the desire of those in power to acquire more power and dominion over others, and to acquire more land and property. As individuals, money is acquired for the sake of, and in the service of the body. And because of all these physical needs, desires, and intrusions we have little time for philosophic contemplation. Even if we are at leisure and have the time for speculation, the body is always bothering us so that we are hindered from seeking the truth. Thus, we make the nearest approach to knowledge when we have the least possible notice of our bodies.

The necessity of eating and drinking, and the fascination with bodily desires and pleasures are so strong and constant from the moment of birth, that the mind is tricked into believing that truth exists only in physical form. The allure that sight and touch and taste and the other senses bring to us in an immediate and powerful form causes us to ignore as useless anything abstract, which to the body is dark and invisible, and can be attained only by constant struggle through philosophical thinking.

Courage is one of the characteristic qualities of a philosopher. Another is temperance, the ability to control and regulate the emotions. The exchange of one fear or pleasure or pain for another fear or pleasure or pain, as if they were coins, is not the exchange of virtue. There is one true coin for which all things ought to be exchanged—wisdom—and only in exchange for this, and in company with this, is anything truly bought or sold, whether courage or temperance or justice or knowledge. Virtue is the companion of wisdom. But a so-called virtue which is severed from wisdom is a shadow of virtue. I have sought wisdom my whole life. I have been seeking according to my ability, and whether I have succeeded or not, perhaps I will know in a little while. Philosophical discussions such as this are not meant to end quickly; we need to think about the issues and the arguments for as long as it takes. Philosophy requires patience and reflection. It is also important that you recognize places in the discussion that seem clear and acceptable, so you can spend more time thinking about what is not yet clear, or where you still have doubts. Also, it is good to sometimes keep moving ahead because added discussion can often help clarify what has already been mentioned. It gives the unconscious part of your mind a chance to ruminate on what you have been consciously thinking about. A great thing about philosophy is that you can jump in anywhere; sooner or later ideas will begin to take shape.

Philosophy requires silent time where we can meditate on what our conversations reveal. Just as food requires time to digest, thoughts need to be digested by our minds. In time, we hope that the nourishment of our thoughts will supply our minds with the necessary requirements. But bad ideas, like bad food, are a real danger to be avoided.

"But how can we recognize bad ideas, Socrates?"

We can't always recognize bad food. We usually have to wait until the poison gets into our bloodstreams—of course, we hope that it is not fatal. Bad ideas might take longer to recognize; it depends on how they affect our lives. As with most things, long experience helps to reveal the good and the bad in every field. But do not fear doubt. Much of what we do is basic exploration; we put one foot forward and then another, not always sure where this will lead.

I know that doubt is like a wound that could fester if untreated; but passionate questioning and longing to know is a healing process. Do not become a misologist—someone who hates or distrusts the use of reason or argument. Where a misanthropist hates or distrusts humankind, a misologist hates or distrusts ideas or the reasoning process. In fact, both spring from the same cause, which is ignorance of the world. Misanthropy arises out of the foolish confidence of inexperience—we trust someone and then in a little while our belief is dashed, and when this has happened several times, especially when it happens among those we think to be our trusted friends, we at last hate and distrust all humans, and we believe that no one is any good at all. This is based on a simple error of judgment, a too hasty conclusion without surveying more of the world. A more expansive view of human nature through more experience would show the truth. Similarly, when a person who has little or no skill in reasoning believes an argument to be correct, which he afterwards believes to be incorrect—whether really incorrect or not—and then another and another, he no longer has any faith in reason. The misologist loses all hope of finding truth and knowledge. But think how sad it would be if there were no such things as truth and the possibility of knowledge.

We need to be careful of allowing into our minds the notion that there is no correctness or truth in any argument at all. Rather, let us say that we have not yet attained correctness or truth; that we must struggle mightily and do our best to gain a healthy mind—you and all others in the rest of your life, and I myself in the prospect of death. For at this moment, I am aware that I may not have the temper of a philosopher; that being so near to death I may have become merely a partisan. And partisans, when they are engaged in disputes, care nothing about the rights of the question at hand, but are anxious to convince others of their assertions. But perhaps the difference between them and me at the present moment is simply this—that whereas they seek to convince others that what they say is true, I am seeking to convince myself. And see how much I gain by the argument. For if what I say is true, then I do well to be persuaded of the truth. But if there is nothing after death, still, during the short time that remains, I shall not distress my friends with expressions of sorrow or grief. My ignorance will not last; it will die with me, and no harm will be done.

This is the state of mind in which I find myself. And I ask you to think of the truth, and not of Socrates. Agree with me, if I seem to be speaking the truth; or if not, then continue to argue and converse with all your intelligence, so that I may not deceive you as well as myself in my enthusiasm, and like the bee, leave my sting in you before I die.

I can see by your faces that you are still feeling an uncertainty because of the greatness of the subject and your inability to comprehend every point. I understand your feelings. Do not despair. When the reasoning process has been shown to be correct, then, with a hesitating and humble confidence in human reason, you may, I think, finally come to accept the course of an argument. And if that happens, and if everything is clear, then you will have done your best. No one can ask for more.

Many people heard me talk over the years, and yet when they relate what I said to others, although they might get my words right, their interpretations of what I meant go in different directions. I suspect that they are not necessarily at fault. For instance, I might say something about a topic by way of an example, but then I might use a different example or offer a slightly different explanation at another time. Those who follow me around are unlikely to have been present at every conversation that I had. After all, I have been talking to people for many years, long before the younger amongst my followers were even born. Also, the nature of a conversation depends on the person I am talking with and how familiar we are with each other's positions.

Someone once said to me that I quite often seem to give merely practical advice instead of direct philosophical teaching. I was amused by the phrase "merely practical advice," as if it were not as important as more general philosophical knowledge. Another person once said that since I gave different advice for different people and situations, this might lead to my giving contradictory advice. I responded by saying that advice pertinent to a specific person—for example a grown person—may not be relevant, and perhaps even harmful, to a young person. Giving different advice in those cases is not contradictory. It is also likely that some of my thoughts and arguments have undergone changes over time, especially since I devote my life not only to cross-examining other people's beliefs, but in self-examination as well. Perhaps after I am gone some of my young friends will decide to carry on with philosophy. I hope they continue to do so, and that their efforts are successful.

Now that the time is near, some of you are anxious to hear my thoughts on what to do with my body. Do whatever you wish, but you must get hold of me and take care that I do not run away from you.

I see that some of you cannot believe that I am the same Socrates who has been talking and discussing the same old topics. You look at me as the Socrates you will soon see, a dead body. But I ask you not to grieve for my body. When the time comes, I shall leave you. ≈ ≈ ≈ ≈

After a few minutes had passed from Socrates's final spoken words to Crito regarding the payment of the debt to Asclepius, the last breath of Socrates left his body.

NOTES

The scenes of Socrates's reveries were created by imagining Socrates's internal thoughts in the last few moments before his death. Although this creation was inspired by some of the works of Plato and Xenophon, nevertheless, *The Hemlock Dialogues* is a work of fiction.

This book offers a fresh reworking of Socrates's thoughts to reveal a remarkably relevant life devoted to helping others strive for clear thinking and ethical behavior. Readers who are unfamiliar with Socrates might doubt that his life and thoughts are relevant to today's world. I hope that this book will encourage readers to explore more of Socrates's thoughts and life by reading some of the writings of Plato and Xenophon, as well as some of the numerous biographies of Socrates.

The following is offered as a guide to the dialogues that inspired the imaginary reveries of Socrates depicted in this book.

The beginning two paragraphs on page 5, and the end paragraph on page 185:
Plato, *Phaedo.* Translated by Benjamin Jowett, 1892.

Socrates's defense at his trial, pages 6-25:
Plato, *Apology.* Translated by Benjamin Jowett, 1892.

Xenophon, *The Apology.* Translated by H. G. Dakyns, 1897.

Xenophon, *Memorabilia*. Translated by H. G. Dakyns, 1897.

Socrates's counter-proposal at the trial, pages 26-27:

Plato, *Apology*. Translated by Benjamin Jowett, 1892.

Xenophon, *The Apology*. Translated by H. G. Dakyns, 1897.

Socrates's final statement at trial, pages 28-31:

Plato, *Apology*. Translated by Benjamin Jowett, 1892.

Xenophon, *The Apology*. Translated by H. G. Dakyns, 1897.

Accusations that Socrates purposely tried to lose his case, pages 31-49:

Xenophon, *The Apology*. Translated by H. G. Dakyns, 1897.

Xenophon, *Memorabilia*. Translated by H. G. Dakyns, 1897.

Euthyphro and Hippias, pages 50-72:

Plato, *Euthyphro*. Translated by Benjamin Jowett, 1892.

Xenophon, *Memorabilia*. Translated by H. G. Dakyns, 1897.

Euthydemus, pages 73-89:

Xenophon, *Memorabilia*. Translated by H. G. Dakyns, 1897.

Pericles: pages 89-97

Xenophon, *Memorabilia*. Translated by H. G. Dakyns, 1897.

Discussions of *function*, *purpose*, **and** *piety*, **but in practical terms**—*doing* **and** *actions,* **pages 97-101:**

Xenophon, *Memorabilia.* Translated by H. G. Dakyns, 1897.

Piety and what is beneficial, pages 101-107:

Xenophon, *Memorabilia.* Translated by H. G. Dakyns, 1897.

Critobulus and Ischomachus, pages 107-135:

Xenophon, *Memorabilia.* Translated by H. G. Dakyns, 1897.

Meno, pages 135-151:

Plato, *Meno.* Translated by Benjamin Jowett, 1892.

Ring of Gyges, pages 151-164:

Plato, *Republic.* Translated by Benjamin Jowett, 1892.

Crito, pages 164-176:

Plato, *Crito*. Translated by Benjamin Jowett, 1892.

Socrates's final thoughts, pages 176-185:

Plato, *Phaedo.* Translated by Benjamin Jowett, 1892.